Diamond Presence

Diamond Presence

Twelve Stories of Finding God
at the Old Ball Park

Edited by Gregory F. Augustine Pierce
Foreword by John Dewan

ACTA
PUBLICATIONS

Diamond Presence
Twelve Stories of Finding God at the Old Ball Park
edited by Gregory F. Augustine Pierce
with a foreword by John Dewan

Cover design and photo by Tom A. Wright
Typesetting by Desktop Edit Shop, Inc.
Cover photo of Oriole Park at Camden Yards in Baltimore, Maryland,
used under rights granted to Seescapes Publishing

Published by: ACTA Publications
                 4848 N. Clark Street
                 Chicago, IL 60640-4711
                 773-271-1030
                 www.actapublications.com

Library of Congress Catalog Number: 2004110375
ISBN: 0-87946-270-1
Printed in the United States of America
Year: 10 09 08 07 06 05 04
Printing: 10 9 8 7 6 5 4 3 2 1

Contents

Dedication

To Bill and Mary Frances Veeck,
in whom God is well pleased.

Foreword

by *John Dewan*
Owner of Baseball Info Solutions

'**I**'ve spent most of my career working with sports information, especially baseball statistics, but *Diamond Presence* has shown me some of the deeper spiritual significance of the game.

I remember when our son Jason was about six months old and my wife and I took him to a baseball game at old Comiskey Park. Since the White Sox were clients of my sports information company, we lucked out and got some really good seats (much like Jean Larkin did in her story in this book).

We were literally right next to the on-deck circle, and it was fascinating to see how the players conducted themselves there during the game. Carlton Fisk, for example, was all business, completely focused on the pitcher every second. Ozzie Guillen, on the other hand, seemed to be on deck not to prepare for his at-bats but to interact with the fans. He was constantly turning towards the stands, waving at his family, friends and fans in general.

During one of Ozzie's times on deck, the Sox were rallying and the fans were really getting into it. The noise level went way up, which was great fun to most of us, but to Jason this kind of cheering and shouting was something new and scary. Suddenly he began to cry for all he was worth. To our great amazement, Ozzie turned around while still in the on-deck circle and began to console our son, right in the middle of the game!

His words of encouragement connected at some level, I'm sure, with our six-month-old son, but Ozzie's other child-consolation technique—poking Jason with his bat—had the opposite effect. Jason began to cry even harder. But this did not phase Ozzie. Next thing we knew, he ducked into the dugout and came out with a ball in his hand. He gave it to Jason and then strode to the plate.

I can't remember whether or not Ozzie got a hit (you could find out in one of the statistics books I published), but I'll never forget that gesture. We later got the ball signed by him and to this day it is still one of Jason's most prized possessions, even though he is now a teenager. For years after that wonderful day at the park, every time he saw Ozzie Guillen, now the manager of the Sox, he asked, "He's the one who gave me the ball, right Dad?"

And I always said, "Yeah, that's right, Jason."

You see, Jason doesn't remember that day at the ballpark when he was less than a year old. What he remembers is the countless times I pointed out Ozzie Guillen as the baseball player who gave him the ball.

—

The stories you will read in *Diamond Presence* are about how baseball is able to capture what life is really all about: joy and beauty and loyalty and teamwork and courage...and giving a crying little boy a baseball. As Fr. Pat Hannon says in his story, "I go to churches and ballparks for pretty much the same reason: because God is there."

God is found in every part of baseball. He's on the field as the heart and soul of a ballplayer, like Billy Joe Barrett in Andre Dubus' story or Bob Raccuglia playing his single game with Greg Luzinski. He's in the stands as the fan who simply loves to be there, like Fr. Bill Fitzgerald. He's in the beauty of the ivy at Wrigley Field for Pat Reardon and his Uncle Eddie. He's even in the incredible richness, complexity and fun of the statistics of baseball. (I can personally attest to that one.) I want to thank Ozzie Guillen and the authors of *Diamond Presence* for reminding me that God is, in fact, everywhere.

Introduction

by Gregory F. Augustine Pierce

H ow do we humans experience the Presence of God in our lives? That quest is certainly the goal of all spirituality. But what if some of us experience that Divine Presence sometimes—not all the time, and certainly not exclusively, but some of the time—at the "old ball park"? Wouldn't that experience change the way we watch, coach and root for our favorite teams? I experienced this kind of Diamond Presence as I coached little boys in the great game of baseball, and I never looked at sports—or spirituality—the same way again.

Over a ten-year period I must have coached fifteen different baseball teams for the Edgebrook Sauganash Athletic Association (E.S.A.A.) in our neighborhood on the northwest side of Chicago, eventually ending up with a three-year stint as a board member and the "commissioner" of the hardball "major league," which was for ten- and eleven-year-old boys in the sixth and seventh grades. It was the final level that the boys played in the summer before they went off to high school.

I have to admit that I coached mostly for me. I loved coaching little kids, teaching them the basics of hitting ("back foot planted, eye on the ball, short step, snap your wrists"), fielding ("ready position, knees bent, mitt on the ground") and running the bases ("three-sidestep lead every pitch, ready to explode, slide unless I tell you to stay up").

I coached all three of my kids, but eventually Abby migrated into softball and other sports instead. So I stuck with Nate and Zack until they both went off to high school. Then I officially "retired" from coaching, figuring I would let other fathers (and mothers) have as much fun as I had enjoyed.

Before I retired from coaching, however, an incident occurred that revealed to me a deeper, spiritual level of coaching...and of the game of baseball itself.

Now, you have to understand that the championship game of the major league of E.S.A.A. is the high point not only of the season but also of the entire baseball career of most of the boys. Many of them quit organized baseball altogether after this year, and those who go on to play in high school are no longer playing with their tee-ball buddies. It is even more bittersweet for the fathers who have been coaching their sons for years and know that after this game they will be relegated back to the dread status of "parent" on the ball field, where all you are supposed to do is cheer for your kid's team and keep your mouth shut about your evaluation of the various players' relative talent and what strategies *you* think the coach should employ.

So the championship game that particular year was a big deal for me, since I knew my older son Nate would be leaving the league and I would never coach him again. Our team, the Dodgers, had come in fifth out of seven teams in the regular fourteen-game season. We had played okay during the year, but I had a philosophy of playing all the kids at least two innings in the infield each game, and that meant we lost a lot of games early in the season because the weaker players could not always make the play. But it did allow all of the boys to feel that they were an important part of the team and not just stuck in the outfield all the time. Plus, this system allowed all the boys to actually learn the game of baseball, even if they did not go on to play it in high school. (Hey, they might want to coach *their* kids when they grow up and get married!)

In the playoffs at the end of the season, however, the Dodgers came together. The format of the playoff tournament was "double-elimination," which means that once you lose two games you're out. The Dodgers won a couple of games against teams that had finished higher in the standings, then we lost a game, but then we won all the remaining playoff games to get to the championship game from what is known as the "loser's bracket."

Even more remarkably, however, the team that won the "winner's bracket," which means that they won *all* of their playoff games, was the Reds. The Reds had finished dead last during the regular season, winning only one game on the way to a 1-13 record. But somehow the Reds, much like the Dodgers, had turned it on in the playoffs, beating everyone—including the Dodgers.

So these were the two teams who met on Saturday, July 15, 2000, for the championship game of the E.S.A.A. boys major league: the seventh-place Reds vs. the fifth-place Dodgers. The Reds were the home team, because they had come out of the winner's bracket, and the Dodgers were the visitors. What's more, the rules stated that should the Reds lose, a second game would have to be played the next day, since it was a "double elimination" tournament and they had yet to lose a game.

I'm not going to bore you with the details of the game, but two significant things occurred that have made me view baseball in a different light ever since.

First, the Reds' best pitcher, one of the kids who had really stepped it up in the playoffs and gotten the team to the championship game, threw out his arm. I had never seen this happen in my ten years of coaching, but right in front of all of us little Danny Kearns threw a pitch that went sailing high over the catcher's mitt to the backstop. When he tried to throw the next pitch, Danny's arm was like a rag. He couldn't even lob it to the catcher. Of course he had to come out of the game.

The Dodgers were ahead at the time, but after the injury the game was all but over. Anyone who has coached in a "house league" at this level knows there are not enough decent pitchers to go around. If you've got two good pitchers, you're happy. Of course, we would have to play again the next day, but without Danny Kearns the Reds were done, and everyone knew it.

Before the final inning, however, I did something that was controversial but is probably one of the best things I have ever done...not only on a ball field but in my life.

I went over to the two Reds' coaches and said, "I'll make you a deal. If you win the game, you will be the champions—obviously. If we win the game, however, rather than play tomorrow without Danny Kearns let's declare that we are co-champions." It took them about two seconds to agree, since they had little to lose. We then played the final inning, telling no one of our "deal."

The Dodgers were ahead 7-2 in the bottom of the last inning, but the Reds made a comeback, scoring two runs and having the bases loaded with two outs when their batter hit a hard grounder to the Dodger first baseman, Paul Weaver. Paul was one of our younger players, one of the boys I had coached several times over the years (always playing him at least two innings in the infield), and his fielding had improved enough that he could now play first base pretty well. He snared the grounder, beat the runner to first, and the Dodgers won the game. Everyone assumed there would be a second game the next day and that the Dodgers would certainly win, given the injury to Danny Kearns. Instead the Reds' and the Dodgers' coaches jointly announced that we were going to share the championship. Both teams were winners; both teams were "number one."

—

I then huddled with my Dodger players. While they were excited at having won the game, they were upset that I had agreed to cancel the next game. They felt they would win, especially if the other team didn't have Danny Kearns, and they wanted to be the clear and only champs.

I admit I was a little taken aback and even doubted myself for a minute. The kids had worked hard. They should feel happy, not disappointed. Maybe they did deserve to play the final game. But I stuck to my guns. "No," I told them, "this is the right thing to do. We are still champions, even though they are too."

The boys, including my own son, did not buy this argument, but most of the parents and coaches on both teams (and on other teams that were watching as well) understood and appreciated what had happened. We then handed out championship trophies to both the Reds and the Dodgers.

"I hope that when you grow up and look back on this, you'll understand," I whispered to Nate as I handed him his trophy.

—

A couple of years later, I got a call from Paul Weaver's mother. She wanted to take my picture for an eighth-grade project her son had written. It was supposed to be on a person that had inspired him, and he had chosen me. Here is some of what Paul wrote:

Greg Pierce has been my baseball coach for four years. Mr. Pierce has had a substantial impact on me by teaching me baseball skills and good sportsmanship; he has fostered good relationships with other players and their families, he has taught me good leadership skills, and he has been instrumental in building self-esteem and motivation....

I am most grateful for the emphasis and importance Mr. Pierce has placed on teaching us about teamwork. He felt that it was more important for us to value working together as a team than on our individual successes. In this capacity, he fostered positive and strong relationship between players. There are many times through this process that I know Mr. Pierce was frustrated with us because he thought we weren't valuing this important message, but we did, and we know that we will be better for it....

—

It was only when I read this essay, by one of the hundred or more kids I had coached over those years, that I knew for sure that the Divine Presence truly had been with me on the baseball field, giving me the wisdom and the courage to act in the way I know I should. I wondered if others had had similar experiences of finding God in the midst of the great game of baseball—as players, coaches, fans or observers. I asked some of my favorite writers to contribute their stories:

Patrick Hannon has carried on a lifelong love affair...with the Oakland A's. "It was my mother who carried me into Our Lady of Grace Church for the first time when I was a baby, and she was the one who took me to my first Oakland Athletics baseball game," he writes. "I don't remember my first day of church, but I do remember my first trip to the ballpark on Heggenberger Road just off the Nimitz Freeway in Oakland, California."

Robert Raccuglia recalls a single high school baseball game that climaxed his season of a lifetime. "When Coach Burke called me up to varsity toward the end of my sophomore season," he says, "I felt thrilled to be rewarded in this way for the good year I was having, but I did not expect to actually *play*. The pantheon of our school's senior players included baseball god Greg Luzinski, who later played in the major leagues. I didn't belong in the same universe, let alone on the same field. Nonetheless, for the Catholic league championship game, I found my name penciled in to start at third base. It was 1968 and everything else in the world seemed to be turning upside down, so why should anything surprise me?"

Sara Kaden, who maintains a Website on her personal hero, Lou Gehrig, sees baseball as a metaphor for her relationship with her father. "For all the enjoyment I found in the game, baseball was never much more to me than a form of entertainment on a secluded farm. Dad asked me once when I was little if I wanted to sign up to play in a summer league. I said no. He didn't ask again. That 'no' stood until my second year of high school when my friends finally convinced me to play girls' summer softball."

Patrick T. Reardon watched Cubs games with his Uncle Eddie. "Uncle Eddie didn't seem to notice that he was listening to a different drummer," Reardon recalls. "He sat there with me watching George Altman run in from center field to snare a line drive or grimacing as Dick Ellsworth gave up a home run in the bottom of the eighth. And he enjoyed himself. With him, I came to understand the meditative nature of baseball. It is a game that moves slowly enough that, as a viewer, you have time to think. You have the opportunity to wonder why the manager chose to pinch-hit at this particular moment, or whether the first baseman should be playing in front of the runner with a left-handed batter now at the plate."

Helen Reichert Lambin remembers the spring when she turned twelve. "What we played could be called 'sandlot baseball' only by the most generous definition," she insists. "But I almost hit a home run, broke a neighbor's window, and learned important lessons about honor, laws of physics, growing old...and about boys."

Michael Wilt loves the "story lines" of baseball: "Stories of second and third chances, of letdowns and comebacks, of goats today who are heroes tomorrow. Stories of players who get it done on the field and then show up at a schoolyard or playground to make a difference in the lives of some kids. Even stories of guys who make it very big and then fall very far, subject just like the rest of us mortals to human foibles and weaknesses and addictions. Stories that ain't over till they're over, and even then...."

Jean Larkin is a baseball fan today partly because of the lessons the game has taught her. "I have no idea how many key moments occur in our lifetime," she reflects, "but I know that every day we provide key moments for one another—whether it's at home or work, in church or the mall, on the schoolyard or the baseball diamond. We've all been picked for the team. We all get our turns at bat. Sometimes we hit the ball out of the park. Sometimes we miss it altogether. Sometimes we give it to a little boy. But it's important that we all stay in the game, because we can't win without one another. Life is a team effort."

William John Fitzgerald reminisces about being taken to his first major league game by his father. It was the St. Louis Browns against the Philadelphia A's, and he remembers seeing not only Connie Mack next to the dugout but also General Douglas MacArthur in the stands. "I didn't know what an 'epiphany' was," he says, "but my entrance into that ballpark was an experience so luminous that it hinted at glory—even divine glory."

Carol DeChant describes how her father finds solace in baseball, even as he mourns the death of his wife of seventy years. His focus is on the feats of endurance and skill on the field, and to him the current obsessions with statistics and money in sports is totally beside the point. "At ninety-two, a baseball fan lives for the sacrifice of the present moment," she says. "Nurses come into Dad's room and find him watching ESPN. 'What's the score, Doc?' they ask. And Dad replies, 'I don't know the *score*, I'm watching the *game*.'"

Andre Dubus died several years ago. He was a passionate fan of baseball and wrote one of his best stories about the deep meaning he found in the game (in this case on a minor league field). The team was the Lafayette Brahman Bulls in the Class C Evangeline League in 1948, and Dubus was eleven years old. He tells of the players he worshipped who would never make it to the major leagues and of the player-manager Harry Strom, who simply loved the game. "When Harry looked at me across the table, he was not looking at my body and into my soul and deciding I would never be a ballplayer, he was not focusing on my trifling error on that long day of the clinic. He was looking at my young hope and seeing his own that had propelled him into and kept him in this vocation, this game he had played nearly all his life."

Jerome D. Lamb tells about the funeral of Roger Maris in Fargo, North Dakota, in 1985, a story that somehow captures the deep connection between baseball and real life. "Maybe the significance of the Maris burial was that it somehow bridged the gap between 'us' and 'them,'" he muses. "He was certainly one of them, the superb athlete whose gifts—strength, speed, stamina, grace and a dozen other things—

were meant to bloom in a bigger garden than we have around here, with a longer growing season. But still he was part of here. For years Roger Maris has remained a distinctly un-asteriskable presence in Fargo."

Finally, **Michael Leach** sums up the spiritual nature of baseball. "Heaven begins on the spot you're standing," he says, "and baseball teaches you that. Baseball taught me that God comes to us when we least expect it: in the present moment. I first knew God (without knowing I knew God) playing softball. It took only a moment. And then it was gone. I was eight or nine years old. Maybe ten. It doesn't matter. Because when it happened, time stood still and I was eternal."

Are these stories silly or childish or at least theologically naïve? I don't think so. The holy, the transcendent, the sacred, the divine can be experienced on the baseball field, just as truly as it can in church, on a mountaintop, or at the birth of a child.

The old *Baltimore Catechism* that Catholics used to have to memorize in their youth put it simply. On page two, question two asked: "Where is God?" The answer was as short as it was profound: "God is everywhere."

If God is everywhere, then those of us who love baseball know that God would never miss the opportunity to spend a few hours at the old ball park. Sit back and enjoy these stories by twelve people who discovered that Diamond Presence.

The Banjo Man

by Patrick Hannon

I go to churches and ballparks for pretty much the same reason: because God is there. You'd think that this admission would cause my sainted Irish-Catholic mother to roll in her grave, but really she's the one to blame. It was my mother who carried me into Our Lady of Grace Church for the first time when I was a baby, and she was the one who took me to my first Oakland Athletics baseball game. I don't remember my first day of church, but I do remember my first trip to the ballpark on Heggenberger Road just off the Nimitz Freeway in Oakland, California. It was on a Wednesday night in July 1968. That evening of grace and baseball is stitched into my memory forever.

My mother took me to see the new Oakland A's play Denny McLain's Tigers that warm night because I was apparently the only one of her brood who deserved to go. At least that's what I inferred as we drove together to pick up her younger brother, my Uncle Jim, before we met up with another aunt and uncle at the ballpark. All the way to my Uncle Jim's, my mother was spitting fire. God only knows what my miscreant siblings had done, but I distinctly remember my mother looking over at me in the passenger seat, her sanity hanging from a thread, and saying with her weary eyes, "You, Patrick, you are my last hope."

Long ago I had concluded I was my father's favorite. Now, apparently, I was my mother's as well!

My brothers and sisters might take issue with this remembrance, but they weren't there. As God is my witness, my mother—gripping the steering wheel with white knuckles, her diminutive frame leaning forward as if she were steeling herself for the final battle—bestowed on me a gift that I could only have concluded then (as I do now) was meant for the One Who Was Chosen. No longer could my brothers tease me into a fight by insisting I was adopted. Long ago I had concluded I was my father's favorite. Now, apparently, I was my mother's as well!

And then there was this crazy bearded man with a banjo. I never knew his name. Never knew where he lived. Never knew a single thing about him except that he wore a scraggly red beard that cascaded down to his knees (or so it seemed); that he wore a cape with a huge, Kelly-green calligraphied "A's" stitched onto a golden satin background; and that he played the banjo like nobody's business. I saw him there at the ballpark hundreds of times since that night in 1968, but the first time I laid eyes on him I literally ran into him, or he into me. I had raced ahead after surrendering my ticket to the lady at the turnstile, so excited was I to breathe for the first time the fragrances only baseball parks can produce: the smells of hot dogs and cotton candy and spilled beer, of fresh sod and half-smoked cigars and wooden bleachers. I was so transfixed by those first whiffs of professional baseball, and my gaze was so affixed on the green diamond unfolded before me, that I never saw him coming until he landed on top of me.

He was leaning over me with this goofy grin, his beard nearly touching my chin and his banjo pointed at me like a machine gun. I did what any self-respecting eight-year old would do in such a situation: I screamed as loud and as long as I could. My mother and her siblings were there in an instant and correctly sized up the harmlessness of the situation. My Uncle Jim helped me up, and then he, my mom, my Aunt Rose and my Uncle Bernard had a good laugh at my expense. Me? I couldn't take my eyes off of this hairy lunatic. If I allowed myself one unguarded moment, I was convinced he would snatch me. He'd tie a leash around me and I would become his circus monkey.

I clung to my mother until the beard with the banjo disappeared. But I knew he was there, somewhere in that great expanse of a ballpark. One moment he was up on the third deck entertaining section 315, and then in an instant he was dancing on the roof of the visitor's dugout. If I blinked he'd be standing right in front of me. So I didn't blink.

Only when banjo-man was out of my view could I watch the game. From our right field perch I was able to enjoy for the first time the cocky, surefooted trot of Reggie Jackson as he chased down and caught a deep fly on the run. I got to witness for the first time Campy Campaneris' menacing crouch at the plate daring the pitcher to sneak one past him. I observed Captain Sal Bando's blue-collar work ethic lived out at third base. I was there as Denny McLain notched his eighteenth victory on his way to an amazing thirty-one-win season. It was like opening one present after another, each one more amazing and awe-inspiring than the last. On that July evening, however, most of my energies were focused on watching out for the caped phantom.

—

It was as if a phantom was stalking the whole nation that year as well. 1968 was a tough year. Martin Luther King, Jr. had been silenced by the assassin's bullet. I remember standing outside on our front porch that April looking out onto our street simmering in an unnatural silence and wondering to myself if the world had gone a little crazy. I remember being awakened by my mother in the middle of the night that June. She was visibly shaken and in tears. She had roused all of us to tell us that Bobby Kennedy had been shot. There was the war in Vietnam going at full throttle, and the protesters camping out at People's Park in downtown Berkeley stopped traffic and burned flags and raised the blood pressure of the nation. There were race riots and labor strikes and daily body counts. I honestly don't know how my parents were able to keep it together. That summer I think they mostly took their kids to the ballpark. There it didn't matter if you were a Democrat or Republican, black or white, man or woman, adult or child. The graceful language of baseball muted all the vitriol, and its grit and grace transcended all the ugliness.

> *The graceful language of baseball muted all the vitriol, and its grit and grace transcended all the ugliness.*

For a few hours on a summer's weeknight or weekend, you got to loosen just a little the grip that fear had on you. You could get into a heated argument with a stranger sitting next to you in the bleachers and not worry that it would end in fisticuffs. You argued over a blown call at third or the idiotic move on the manager's part to yank his starting pitcher or the price of beer. And then Rick Monday or Danny Cater would park one in the left field bleachers and everyone would be hugging each other and slapping five and cheering the home team. There was an adrenaline rush, a surge of hope, and for a while we got to enjoy and celebrate what is best about us as human beings. Tomorrow's headlines would be tomorrow's headlines. For that moment, it was enough to be carried by the tide of simple human joy.

The Irish poet Patrick Kavanaugh said it well: "God is in the bits and pieces of Everyday—a kiss here and a laugh again, and sometimes tears, A pearl necklace round the neck of poverty." Going to the ballpark that summer was the pearl necklace we hung around our necks of poverty. It helped us enjoy the gifts of life and pay no heed to the phantom of fear.

I think it might have been during the seventh inning. McLain was working on his shutout and the vendors were racing up and down the aisles barking and begging and selling their wares. From what my Uncle Jim told me later, it began with a peanut. Someone a few rows up had tossed a peanut in the air, and it landed on the head of someone a few rows down from us. We were right in the middle. I remember having this eerie sense that someone had turned the thermostat up. It must have been the immediate tension created by the first peanut, then the angry, irritated glance up and back to see who had thrown it, then a guffaw and giggle and an "Ah, shut up and turn around, you stupid niggers."

I was eight years old, and though I had heard of the "N"

From what my Uncle Jim told me later, it began with a peanut.

word, I had never actually heard it spoken. Hearing it for the first time was like getting slapped across the face—with a shovel. I could only imagine what the black kids below us were thinking and feeling.

Then came another peanut. And another. And another.

It was raining peanuts. Above us was a collection of ten or twelve white guys in their twenties. They seemed thoroughly pleased with themselves. Below us were four or five black kids of high school age. The growing anger—and danger— in the situation was palpable, as it became quickly apparent that we were about to have a racial fight on our hands.

As I look back on it now, I would have hoped that all the adults around us would have stepped up and diffused the situation. But that didn't happen. Most folks—my mom and her brothers and sister included—were caught off guard. Their first reaction was much like mine: mouths wide open in disbelief. But there were others, more than a few, who actually were enjoying the unfolding drama, seeing it, tragically, as a comedy.

I'd like to be able to say that there was no fight—that calmer heads prevailed—but that wouldn't be true. Punches were thrown. Blood was spilt. I was terrified, because the fighting converged on those of us unlucky enough to be in the middle. It was nasty and it was visceral. The phantom of fear wrapped its clammy fingers around our necks once more. But it could have been much worse.

At first I could barely hear the cheerful, buoyant picking of the banjo. But it grew louder and stronger and more insistent. The lunatic with the beard was upon us before the security guards, and his eyes were wild and sad and cast in a light of urgency. Cheering erupted all around us to welcome this holy minstrel, who cut a farcical, ridiculous pose with his cape and long beard but came armed for battle. He played his banjo like I have never seen anyone play a musical instrument since. People started clapping and stomping to the beat, and that gave him the strength and courage to play on.

Slowly, one fighter, then another, then another looked up, punches halted in mid-release like in some Road Runner cartoon. Within half a minute, the warring factions disentangled and disengaged. Arms were grabbed, breaths were caught, steps were taken back from the edge, and a modicum of dignity and decency was restored. By the time banjo-man was finished picking and strumming, sweat was rolling down his forehead and cheeks and collecting in his beard. The entire section of the park erupted in a sustained cheer that seemed to me to shake the very heavens. The man with the banjo took a bow, and then started the cheer, "Let's go A's! Let's go A's! Let's go A's!" And within a minute the whole stadium reverberated with the echo of a new battle cry. Division had been routed; unity had been restored—at least for that one night.

For me the events of that game, from the moment I collided with the banjo player to that thunderous cheer, left me in a state of transfigured awe. It had been the wildest experience of my short life. Kafka wrote about having been filled once with a sense of endless astonishment at simply seeing a group of people cheerfully assembled. As I leaned against the railing looking out onto the Coliseum later that night, having witnessed both the grace and the gravity of the human condition, that partisan cheer washed over me like the waters of baptism, initiating me into a community of faith whose bible was baseball. I realized that I now belonged to a family built on loyalty and faith, a family that lived and died for The Game, and didn't care what else you believed in or did outside of it.

I see the Oakland Coliseum as a kind of cathedral—yet one more sacred place on the planet where I can encounter God.

So it should come as no surprise to anyone that I see the Oakland Coliseum as a kind of cathedral—yet one more sacred place on the planet where I can encounter God. I did that night in July when I found myself in the right field bleachers of the cathedral on Heggenberger for the first time and felt the clamp of fear around my neck. God came to me that night in a long red beard wearing a cape and playing a banjo, and the din of human ugliness surrendered—as it always must—to the joyful music of grace and peace.

Playing with Luzinski

by Robert Raccuglia

I f ever there was a year to be coming of age in America, 1968 was it. I was a sophomore in high school, awakening to new worlds all around: Olivia Hussey's breathy Juliet made Shakespeare suddenly accessible; Holden Caufield and Atticus Finch were drawing me into the world of literature; Bob Dylan and Joni Mitchell were saying everything that to my teenage mind needed to be said about life. I began learning about Gandhi and nonviolence. Martin Luther King was assassinated. Robert Kennedy was assassinated. People *I knew* were maced outside of the Democratic National Convention.

Amid so much upheaval, one thing remained constant: baseball. It was all I wanted to do every summer since my Uncle Don first taught me to throw and catch a ball.

Having started at second base as a Notre Dame High School freshman, I felt confident of making the team again my sophomore year, but I never expected to improve so dramatically. For me it was the kind of season that I thought could only come from selling your soul to the devil (which, just for the record, I did not do).

When Coach Burke called me up to varsity toward the end of the year, I was as much shocked as thrilled.

Every ground ball that I hit leaked through the infield for a single. If I hit a line drive, it would find a gap and seem to roll forever like a ball bearing on the hard ground, so that I actually found myself sprinting around the bases for a home run more than once. Even when some fastballer overmatched me, I would slice a soft flair to some uncatchable spot in right. All season, I felt the incomparable joy of being totally in the flow of the game.

Still, when Coach Burke called me up to varsity toward the end of the year, I was as much shocked as thrilled. The pantheon of our school's senior players included baseball god Greg Luzinski, who later played in the major leagues. I did not belong in the same universe, let alone on the same field. The only thing that kept me from being utterly terrified was the knowledge that nothing would be expected of me other than to shag some flies in batting practice and cheer the guys on from the bench.

I was not a solid member of the jock fraternity. Basketball and football reigned at our school. I was too short and unskilled for hoops. I did play freshman football, but as a fifth string half back I was not exactly what you would call an "impact player." My one carry all season netted two yards and a bloody nose. When I finally caught a pass (my only reception), I jitterbugged around an oafish linebacker and ran for fifteen yards...before fumbling. I was knocked unconscious once trying to make a tackle in practice drills. Those were the highlights of my gridiron career. (In contrast, Luzinski, in addition to excelling in baseball, had been offered a number of college football scholarships, as had other members of the varsity baseball team.)

Needless to say, my overall athletic reputation did not precede me in my promotion to varsity baseball, or if it did, I wished it hadn't.

—

The first practice went fairly well. I felt awkward and out of place, but enjoyed chasing Luzinski's towering drives and don't remember doing anything to embarrass myself. I knew most of the varsity guys by reputation and had played in a park district league with a few of them. Not too sure of myself, I approached my teammates with appropriate diffidence. Or rather, I did *not* approach them unless they approached me, which meant that I spent most of my time during practice alone in the outfield. But I could not have been happier to be there.

I joined varsity with only a game against Holy Cross left to play. They were a team that we battled perennially for the conference championship in every sport. There was a Yankee-Red Sox feel to the rivalry. Of all of the other schools, Holy Cross was the only one whose players' names were familiar to us—Masciopinto, DiBennedetto, Mariani.... They all had been shaving since sixth grade and, I imagined, most had fathered children by junior year.

So far that school year, our varsity had topped them to claim football and basketball titles. Now the baseball season was coming to a close with Notre Dame and Holy Cross having earned identical records. Early in the spring, they handed us our only conference loss. In our second meeting, a snow storm (a normal hazard of playing baseball in April in Chicago) ended the game in a 6-6 tie. Now the conference scheduled a playoff game to determine the champion.

On the sophomore team, Holy Cross gave us one of only two losses we suffered all year. So for me it was exciting to return to play our toughest adversary once more – this time on varsity with the conference title on the line. It didn't matter that I'd be watching it from the dugout.

The drama heightened when we learned on the day before the game that Danny Murtaugh, former Pittsburgh manager, would be on hand to scout Luzinski for the Pirates.

___

On game day I had little patience for the irrelevancies of Latin, history and math classes. Who cared if *"Omnia Gallia in partes tres divisa est?"* In eighth-period trigonometry, Father Hess interrupted my reverie by demanding, "Mr. Raccuglia, who appointed you vice president in charge of looking out the window?" I didn't know I needed an appointment.

Finally, the school day ended. In deference to my elders, I waited until last to get on the team bus. When I climbed on, someone shouted from the back, "Here comes Jimmy!" It was Luzinski. He knew my name! (Well, it wasn't really my name, but I was grateful for the recognition all the same.) Apparently, Luzinski had decided that, for the day, I would take on the identity of Jimmy Davenport, third base-man of the San Francisco Giants. It turns out that he had already been told the news that the manager had wisely withheld from me: I would be starting at third base.

It turns out that he had already been told the news that the manager had wisely withheld from me: I would be starting at third base.

My mind was racing. Hadn't the sophomore coach informed him about my scatter-armed throws? Didn't he understand that this game meant the championship? Didn't he know that Danny Murtaugh would be in the stands? My inherited Sicilian fatalism began flashing mental previews of the varieties of disaster that lay ahead. I had only the length of the bus ride to Holy Cross to quiet my nerves with a self-administered pep talk. *He wouldn't put you in the game if he didn't think you could do the job. You played well all season; you'll play well today. You can do it!* Unfortunately, the pep talk wasn't working.

During infield practice I looked across the diamond at Luzinski. In his four seasons of varsity play he never batted under .500. Once he hit a ball on our gym roof, a blast measured at more than 460 feet. All week in batting practice I noticed that everyone evacuated the infield when Luzinski came up to take his cuts. Having seen him rifle drives down the line, I was thankful to be playing third on his team and not for the opposition.

I wasn't looking to be a batting hero. I just didn't want to do anything that would cost us the game.

Coach Burke penciled me in the lineup to bat ninth. Normally, I would be insulted to be placed at the end of the order, but in this case it was a relief. I wasn't looking to be a batting hero. I just didn't want to do anything that would cost us the game.

I relaxed a little in the top of the first when we took the lead on a long RBI double by Luzinski. Then we were out in the field. My warm up throws to first were on the mark and I began to think maybe I would get through the game all right. After two quick outs, however, our pitcher, Tom Michalik, allowed a walk and the Holy Cross clean up hitter, a lefty, stepped in. He hit a towering pop up toward third. "Mine! Mine!" I hollered, but I was hoping that our shortstop, Tom Grammarosa, would call me off and take it. The ball kept drifting steadily to my right; it was definitely my play. I moved under the ball, almost at the third base bag, staggered a few quick steps into foul territory, then, heart pounding, made a desperate lunge and caught it. I ended up right in front of our bench, turned, and casually tossed the ball to the mound. Relieved and embarrassed, I accepted the amused congratulations of my teammates. (A catch like that, I realized, would have qualified me for the Don Landrum Award, a mock honor that we invented earlier in the year during the boredom of batting practice. It was named for a Cubs centerfielder who had a knack of making the easy look difficult, and it was given for "the most spectacular catch on a routine fly ball." Messing around during practice, I was always vying for the dubious award, but it wasn't a distinction that I particularly wanted to merit in a real game.)

In my first at bat in the second inning, I worked the pitcher to a full count, fouling off a couple of close pitches before striking out. So far, I had not acquitted myself very well, but I was beginning to feel more at ease.

Holy Cross threatened in the third, putting two men on base. A laser-like throw from our catcher, Ed Miller, picked the runner off second, and the rally failed. It struck me again that my teammates performed on a level that I was not accustomed to playing. *God, these guys are good!*

In the sixth we still held a 1-0 lead. I had a chance to extend our advantage in the top of the inning when I came up with the bases loaded and two outs, but on the first pitch all I managed was an anemic grounder to second. *At least I hit the ball*, I told myself. I grabbed my glove and headed out to field my position. With one out, Holy Cross put the tying run on second with a single and stolen base. On a hit and run, the next batter drilled a one-hopper to Grammarosa. Tom rifled a perfect peg to me at third. The play unfolded so quickly that I realized that I could tag the runner and possibly double up the batter at first. I received the throw and made a hasty premature swipe at the approaching runner who was just beginning his slide. He was still a full three feet from me when I completed the sweeping "tag" and took a hop step to launch a throw to first. My relay reached Luzinski a split second after the batter crossed the bag, but to our amazement—and the Holy Cross team's total disbelief—the umpire signaled a double play.

Except for the fact that neither runner should have been called out, the play looked terrific. Their manager charged the umpire to argue as we trotted off the field to the cheers and laughter of our fans. By then, Danny Murtaugh had left the park.

We scored again and went into the last inning with a slim 2-0 lead. Not wanting to tempt fate, I was praying that Michalik would strike out the side so that no more balls would come my way and we could go home winners. Holy Cross, however, sent up the heart of their order, and their number three hitter led off with a walk. That brought up the clean up batter who (I am not making this up) lofted the exact same sky-high pop up that he hit in the first. And I did the identical manic dance under it and again comically snared it with a last-minute lunge. Coach Burke shook his head slowly with a half-smile on his face, no doubt feeling as relieved as I was. I was a lock for the Don Landrum Award.

Coach Burke shook his head slowly with a half-smile on his face, no doubt feeling as relieved as I was.

Mercifully, the final two outs came quickly and easily. There were high fives all around. Walking off the field, I got a slap on the back from Luzinski. Later that summer he would be drafted in the first round by the Phillies, then go on to have a fifteen-year major league career, hitting more than 300 home runs. My post-high school baseball experience mainly would consist of summer evenings in front of a TV set, but on that day I had teamed up with a future National League All-Star in a championship game, and we won.

It's funny how vivid the memories of that one game are to me even now, especially compared to so many other more significant occurrences that I have long forgotten. That year had been full of momentous, earth shaking events. The play-off game between Notre Dame and Holy Cross was not one of them. It was a little moment, even for those of us caught up in it. But it was a good one.

I was sixteen that year. I wanted to end the war in Vietnam. I wanted to see Dr. King's dream realized. I wanted to get my driver's license. I wanted to get up the nerve to ask girls out. I wanted to play baseball. Somehow, it all fit.

> *There would come a period after high school when I thought baseball was a waste of time for any socially conscious person.*

There would come a period after high school when I thought baseball was a waste of time for any socially conscious person. But I am glad that I did not feel that way in 1968, and I am glad that I do not feel that way now.

Baseball can occupy a big space in a kid's life. It did for me. Since spiritual masters rightfully exhort us to find God in all things, I don't think it is too fanciful to recognize the divine even on the baseball diamond. I can imagine God's pleasure in our pursuit of the wholly useless and enjoyable art of hitting and fielding. There are worse things a kid could do with his time. And there are few that have the power to engage the body, mind and spirit of a young person so completely. So if the famous second century claim of Irenaeus that "The glory of God is a person fully alive!" is true, who's to say that baseball is not among the innumerable ways that we experience the divine presence?

All of our lives are filled with countless avenues of grace, openings to growth that help to define the person we are to become. There are ten thousand ways that life can test and stretch us. Sometimes it is through weighty events, other times through matters of little apparent consequence. They all have their place.

Baseball was a part of my coming of age, as natural as it was fun. I did not have to be Luzinski to find a place on the field. I always felt grateful just to be in the game.

Epilogue

Thirty-six years later, I accompanied a few of my high school classmates, now old guys in their fifties, to watch the 2004 Notre Dame Dons play for the Illinois State Championship. Our team overcame a seven-run deficit to win the semi-final and then came from behind with three late inning runs to take the title game. The day left us hoarse and exhilarated. (Why do women think men don't know how to show emotion?)

My stomach tensed with our batters at every key at bat; my heart pumped with every runner that rounded third to beat the throw home. I gloried in "our" accomplishment. No doubt, three decades from now these kids from Notre Dame, though by then balding and graying, will be able to give an inning-by-inning account of their championship contest as if it were yesterday, because baseball can take hold of you—it's just the nature of the game.

A Smile at Third Base

by Sara Kaden

I used to think my relationship with my father was abnormal. The dads in the McDonald's commercials never seemed to feel uncomfortable or hesitate to express their love for their kids. In my dad, however, visible emotion was always (and remains today) a sparse commodity—and spoken emotion even more rare.

Dad is the product of Depression-surviving farmers. I wondered many times growing up if God forgot to write the smile chromosome in him and his dad and his dad's dad, producing a lineage of straight lips that parted only to eat and yell at cows that wouldn't move. How does a little girl relate to that? I tried being a tomboy to help Dad on the farm, but by the time I grew big enough to carry a full feed bucket, he had enough hired hands and I was left to carry basket loads of wet clothes to the line. When I made the honor roll at school (like he used to do), it only won me the privilege of figuring out my subsequent homework on my own.

This interaction with my father seemed strange to me, unnatural even. I guess I thought that if our relationship wasn't mirrored in the McDonald's commercials then it couldn't be natural. I felt cheated. But then God used a clever vehicle to show me the truth about my dad and me. The vehicle was a smile that Dad gave me one time while I was standing at third base.

—

Baseball was always present in our house in Missouri. One of the few things Dad really liked to do was listen to Jack Buck (the original Hall-of-Fame broadcaster, not his son, Joe) call Cardinals games on the radio. Buck's voice coated the summer breeze coming through the open windows of our home from April through September, and once or twice through a glorious October.

> I remember Dad's chipped catcher's mask and Rawlings glove that we weren't supposed to play with but did anyway.

I remember Dad's chipped catcher's mask and Rawlings glove that we weren't supposed to play with but did anyway. And his wooden softball bats that we weren't suppose to use to hit rocks but did anyway. And the ugly scar on his shoulder from a sliding mishap that he wore like a badge of honor. Our front yard was used exclusively for wiffleball, the plowed-over garden out back for baseball.

I don't remember ever not knowing the foundational rules of baseball. Someone, most likely Dad, taught me them as soon as I learned to walk in grass. For all the enjoyment I found in the game, however, baseball was never much more to me than one of the few forms of entertainment on a secluded farm. Dad asked me once when I was little if I wanted to sign up to play in a summer league. I said no. He didn't ask again.

—

That "no" stood until my second year of high school, when my friends finally convinced me to play girls' summer softball. A handful of games into the summer, it became quite clear to me that our coach knew nothing about the game (a fact Dad had noticed before our first inning of play). So sure enough, Dad offered to help our coach, giving her suggestions for organizing practices and instructions on how to create a lineup. A few more games passed and our coach resigned, asking Dad to take over.

Before he accepted, he asked me if it would be all right. I said okay, thinking this might be the proverbial door I needed to open in order to develop a "normal" (i.e., McDonald's approved) relationship with him. But after he accepted the coaching position, Dad's first statement to me was, "Don't expect special treatment."

—

Always one to take his responsibilities seriously, Dad threw himself into his new role as if it were the fulfillment of a life's dream. New, longer, harder practices that involved base running and bunting and eliminating gossip was his first order of business.

"Why is your Dad so tough?" the girls asked me.

"He really loves the game," I shrugged.

"I only signed up so I wouldn't be bored this summer," one girl said.

"I'm just trying to get a tan on my face," another confided.

"Tell him to stop making us sweat our shoes off," another complained.

"I can't," I shrugged again. "He's the coach." (This truth about baseball I understood instinctively.)

The girls groaned through his first few practices, and some dropped out, but Dad was expecting that. After we started winning games, however, the girls figured out that he knew what he was doing and began enjoying this taciturn man. So they went with the flow.

I too went with the flow—during practice, during games, even when he drilled me on hitting and fielding behind our house for an hour every day after evening chores. Though he tried his hardest, he couldn't break me of my predilection toward throwing sidearm, but he did convince me that a snap and roll of my wrists made for a more powerful swing.

Dad and I spent more time together that one summer than during the prior fifteen years, or so it felt. The more he worked with me, the more I improved, but we didn't discuss it, or really anything else. When he pitched I hit, and when he hit I fielded. That was the way we worked. No sound emanated from our backyard, except clinks from the aluminum bat and the grass swishing under my spikes. No words were exchanged except minimal coach phraseology like "elbow up" and "two hands."

I didn't cry when a grounder he hit took a bad hop and split my lip open; he didn't say whether I was improving or not. We just practiced baseball.

I understood Dad's reasoning behind not treating me differently when the other girls were around.

I understood Dad's reasoning behind not treating me differently when the other girls were around. When I whiffed, I got the same wince the other girls did. When I snagged the final out with flair that resembled a circus catch, I got the same four claps and "good job" he gave all plays that pleased him.

It's fine when a coach treats a player that way, because that's the way a player-coach relationship is supposed to be. But when a father treats his impressionable daughter that way, it has to be at least a little disappointing to her. I was glad to be spending time with my father, but I was spending time with a man who was a bundled package—baseball enthusiast, coach, fan, as well as my father. All the time in the ex-garden field behind our house, Dad didn't do anything with me that he wouldn't have done with any of the girls in team practice. I wanted a part of him that was intended for me only.

—

Every now and again in the grand game of baseball, God's hand descends to empower a single human being to have a defining moment on the playing field: Fisk's ball stayed fair; Mays made the catch over his shoulder and threw out the runner; Gehrig delivered his own eulogy.

It was my turn at the plate. If he gave me a sign, I don't remember it. All I could keep in my mind was, "Base hit drives in a run."

For me, it happened like this. The bases were loaded; it was a close game in a late inning in one of the last games of the season. Dad was pacing in the third-base coach's box, wearing his calm "game face," a couple of his left-hand fingers tucked between his lips. It was my turn at the plate. If he gave me a sign, I don't remember it. All I could keep in my mind was, "Base hit drives in a run," a phrase I had heard him mutter a thousand times while listening to the Cardinal games. The count I don't remember, the pitcher I can't picture. But the low-and-away pitch is as big and fat to me today as it was then. Cling! The ball propelled into deep left, excited cheering erupted on the bench and in the stands. I rounded first and dug for second, glancing over at third for a signal from Dad to stop or go.

To my shock, he was jumping and wildly waving me on. *My father was jumping and waving wildly! My father!* My chest tingled as I fed on his unprecedented (as far as I knew) exhibition of excitement. As I rounded second I could hear him yelling, "Yeah! Yeah!" each time he jumped. I ran faster, pulled forward as if I were caught in the stream of air Dad's arms were pulling towards him.

"That-a-way kid! Way to go! Way to go!"

"Up! Up!" he yelled. I planted my foot on the bag well before the throw arrived. I had hit a stand-up, bases-clearing triple. But I wasn't watching the lights changing on the scoreboard or listening to the standing ovation from the fans. I was experiencing the miracle of my father bounding up to me and slapping me on the back with a half hug and shouting at a volume I didn't know he could, "That-a-way kid! Way to go! Way to go!"

Then he turned to walk back to the coach's box with a last "Yeah!" in the general direction of the bleachers. Before his face turned, though, I observed the smallest big thing he had ever done for me: He was smiling with pride. At that moment I knew he wanted to shout out, "People, I am unbelievably proud of my daughter!"

No one else noticed that little smile, which makes me all the more ecstatic that it happened. He meant for me—and no one else—to notice. The smile was for me alone, and if the course of events had allowed me to retain no other memory of him than this, it would have been enough.

I've often wondered why it was that we connected that particular time. There's really no reason why he should have been so jubilant. I had made good plays before and drew only his standard "Good job." What was it about that game, that hit, that moment? In fact, what was it about baseball that brought us together in a way we never had done before?

It's been said that God shows up in strange places, but we only perceive it that way. God is *always* there, ready to break through the restraints of our human consciousness. God was present to me that day on the ball field. I glimpsed him in my father's smile while I was standing on third base.

Ever since that poignant lesson I've been happier with Dad's subtle expressions of love than with any grand McDonald's-commercial-like gesture he could make. I feel perfectly comfortable with his "Call us when you get there" and our impassioned discussions of the Cardinals' latest game or trade. I now believe our relationship, much like the one I have found with God, is at its healthiest when the little things carry the larger issue.

Ready to Be Caught Off Guard

by Patrick T. Reardon

rnie Banks had this fluid swing that appeared effort-less. His bat would come around in a single motion, meet the ball, and follow through with a beauty that, to my young eyes, seemed classic. He brought to mind the sculptures of Greek athletes and gods I'd seen in my history books. There was grace and rhythm and power. On those frequent occasions when the ball would fly up over the ivy walls of Wrigley Field and out onto Waveland Avenue, Ernie would lope around the bases like a gazelle, with long easy strides and a self-contained joy at being alive.

Originally a shortstop, Ernie had moved over to first base for the 1962 season, the same season I began to watch the Cubs games on a regular basis with my Uncle Eddie.

———

Tony Taylor, Ernie's former double-play partner, had been traded away to the Philadelphia Phillies by then, but he

---

would return to Chicago several times a year to play the Cubs, and I was still fascinated to watch him step into the batter's box.

With his bat under one arm, he would bend slightly from the waist and quickly make the sign of the cross, the same sign of the cross that all of us Catholic children made every morning and often throughout the day, under the watchful eyes of the nuns at St. Thomas Aquinas grammar school on Chicago's West Side. Tony had an added flourish at the end, though. He would place his right thumb over his right forefinger to form a second smaller cross, and kiss this tiny cross. Then he was ready to bat.

As Uncle Eddie and I would watch Cubs games on WGN, Channel 9, there was still a distance between us and the players.

I didn't realize it at the time, but Tony came from Cuba, one of the many heavily Catholic (and baseball-mad) countries of the Caribbean and Central America that over the past forty or fifty years have supplied an ever-increasing number of players to the major leagues. As a twelve year old, I was only vaguely aware of this trend, still in its infancy. Besides, Tony's name didn't sound Spanish.

Sports coverage was in its infancy then as well. As Uncle Eddie and I would watch Cubs games on WGN, Channel 9, there was still a distance between us and the players. Only a handful of cameras were used at the game, primarily one that provided a shot from the centerfield bleachers of the pitcher, catcher and batter, and a second, somewhere behind home plate, that would follow the path of the ball once it was hit. There weren't any of the close-ups that modern sports viewers are used to seeing. You couldn't tell, say, whether Ron Santo had failed to shave that morning. And you couldn't read the lips and expression of Dick Bertell, one of the Cubs catchers, when he'd go to the mound to talk something over with Glenn Hobbie.

What this meant was that Uncle Eddie and I didn't get so caught up in the personalities of the players. Was this guy likeable? Was that guy ornery? We couldn't tell, and the announcers, such as Jack Brickhouse, Lou Boudreau, Vince Lloyd and Lloyd Pettit, didn't enlighten us. Rather than feeling we were in the middle of the action, we saw the batters, pitchers and fielders as if they were on a stage. Later in life, when I began to attend ballets and plays, there was the same feeling of distance. The art was there in front of me to take in without distraction—whether it was a *pas de deux* or a double down the right field line.

I use the word *art* advisedly. Looking back now, I realize that the grace and skill that Ernie Banks displayed—that any major leaguer (even such a ne'er-do-well as Andre Rodgers) was capable of displaying at some point in a game—was a form of artistic expression. It became a doorway for me. Watching baseball with Uncle Eddie, I learned how to take in, enjoy, and savor other forms of creativity. I also came to understand, over the years, that such creativity is, at its heart, spiritual work. It is God's lifeblood.

Physical grace in an athlete is a combination of God's gifts and hard work. It is a metaphor for all of human existence. We take what we are given, and we do something with it. In this sense we are all artists—at least we're all called to be. This was the lesson I began to learn in those years from my Uncle Eddie. In his quiet, unobtrusive way, he helped me open the door to the wider possibilities of life.

—

And he also taught me other lessons as well, like the importance of striving.

There is no such thing in baseball as unalloyed success or failure. Even the worst player on the Cubs in those years—and there were many to choose from, since the Cubs consistently finished at or near the bottom of the standings—would slap a hit through the middle on occasion, or get a called strike on a batter, or nab a deep fly ball. And even Ernie Banks, a future Hall-of-Famer, would make an out two of every three times he came to the plate.

No, the key was the attempt. There were players who, by dogging it and going through the motions, weren't striving; they were taking up space. Most, however, imperfect though their skills might be, tried. They put themselves on the line. They took the risk of swinging hard—and sometimes, many times, struck out. They threw a fastball to a fastball hitter—and sometimes, many times, saw the ball come back in a flash, screaming past their head into center field. But at least they were in the game.

Billy Williams and Glenn Beckert and Fergie Jenkins and the others out there on the field were modeling for me what I needed to do to be fully alive. I needed to be in the game, to make something happen, to take a chance. I needed to take life as I found it and do something with it. I needed to try to have an impact on the world.

I could live my life like these men played baseball, and in a golden moment—with a swing that was just so—I might hit the ball a mile and feel like Ernie Banks. But even if I struck out, even if I grounded into a double-play, I was doing my job, as long as I was trying.

Of course, Ernie and the other Cubs thought they were just playing baseball. They didn't know they were modeling life lessons for me. That's part of what makes dogging it so destructive. Not only are you letting yourself down. You're letting everyone else around you down. You're setting a bad example.

Uncle Eddie set a good example for me, many times over, although I'm sure he never realized it.

Uncle Eddie set a good example for me, many times over, although I'm sure he never realized it.

—

Uncle Eddie was the brother of my mother's mother—my great-uncle. In the early 1960s, he was a widower and my grandmother was a widow. They lived together in a spacious apartment on LeClaire Avenue, about two blocks from my family's home.

Even though I was not yet thirteen, I had nine brothers and sisters. (There would be four more siblings eventually.) I was the oldest. After school each weekday, my brother David or I would be responsible for watching the youngest two or three kids. We alternated days. The job was to get the little kids out of the house to give my mother a breather in which to prepare supper. And, every day, the routine was the same. We'd walk them over to Grandma's apartment and spend an hour or two there.

The job was to get the little kids out of the house to give my mother a breather in which to prepare supper.

When we'd come in, Grandma would offer the little girls—all the youngest kids were girls—some candy from a fancy, cut-glass dish, and then take them into the kitchen where she would be baking a loaf of fresh bread or a batch of thin-crusted, jam-centered kolachkies. Meanwhile, I'd sit down with Uncle Eddie, and, most days, the Cubs game would be on the TV. We'd watch it together. (I'm sure my brother David did the same on his days.)

Uncle Eddie was in his seventies then, and he and I didn't talk much. I wish we had. He'd led an adventurous life, and I never knew more than the barest outlines of it. I don't even remember now what he'd done for a living.

I do know that he served in both World War I and World

War II. He was an American doughboy in Europe in the first war, and when the second one started he tried to enlist again but was told he was too old. So he went to Canada and signed up as an ambulance driver in that nation's army. Again, he ended up back in France.

It wasn't that Uncle Eddie was bloodthirsty. He was a gentle guy. I think he loved the idea of taking part in something big and important. I think he loved the chance to travel the world. I think he liked the idea of fighting for something good.

That's how I read his life then, and how I read it now. It was in sharp contrast to the sort of neighborhood and culture in which I grew up. The St. Thomas Aquinas parish was a generally blue-collar congregation, virtually all Irish Catholic. We were afflicted with the insularity that is often the bane of the Irish in America. There was "us," and there was "them"—the rest of the world. We didn't trust "them." We felt safe and secure only within our clan. We had our church, our God, our community, and we didn't need anything else.

That attitude limited our horizons, to say the least. On some deep level, I was chaffing at those constraints, although I would never have been able, as a good Catholic boy, to acknowledge or articulate my misgivings.

So for me Uncle Eddie's story was a breath of fresh air. I've always thought of it as Hemingway-esque. (Ernest Hemingway grew up in Oak Park, a suburb of Chicago, just a mile west of where my family lived. He left for Europe. He was an ambulance driver in the first world war.) In a neighborhood where no one talked of adventure, Uncle Eddie had lived it.

He was also an inveterate reader. My mother read many books, and Uncle Eddie often would give me books he'd read to bring home to her. But her reading tended to be novels. Uncle Eddie would read, in addition to fiction, many history books.

He saw history as a story—as an adventure. Most of his reading was not a form of escapism but a diving deeper into life. He wanted to understand things. He wanted to see the big picture. He wanted to learn. In that, he's been a model for me. I've tried to teach my two teenage children that learning isn't something that ends when you leave school. It's only beginning then. Learning is essential to living. As long as you're learning—as long as you're striving to understand how life works and how you are called to play a role in the world—you're alive. I've always tried to do that, and only lately I've come to realize that I've been following in Uncle Eddie's footsteps.

Only lately I've come to realize that I've been following in Uncle Eddie's footsteps.

One Christmas we gave him William Shirer's history of the Nazis and Adolf Hitler, *The Rise and Fall of the Third Reich*. It was a hardcover book, and I remember how clear it was to me that this was a big expense on my parents' part. My mother tended to read only paperbacks, but Uncle Eddie, most often, had a hardcover book in his hands. My parents said it was because his eyes were failing and he needed the larger type, but as someone who later in my life came to know the delight of handling a well-made, substantial book with real heft and presence, I think Uncle Eddie read hardcover books because he enjoyed them. They gave him pleasure, and if it meant paying more for them he was willing to cut back on other spending.

He was trying to make art, and if the result was boring, well, at least he'd tried.

Pleasure, in those days, was something generally feared and distrusted by Catholics, particularly Irish Catholics. I heard many a lecture by the nuns and many a sermon by the priests on the dangerousness of pleasure of just about any kind. But Uncle Eddie didn't seem to have those anxieties. He liked what he liked.

His movie camera, for instance. When eight-millimeter cameras (forerunners of today's camcorders) began to come into private use on a wide scale, Uncle Eddie was one of the first buyers. He took a lot of home movies of us because we were kids and we were hams, and it's hard to take bad pictures of kids hamming it up. In an attempt to be artsy, Uncle Eddie took some truly bad, out-of-focus rolls of nothing but the flowers in a backyard garden. These always provoked groans among us kids when they'd come on in the midst of some long reel that he had spliced together. I was one of the groaners. But, even then, I recognized what he was trying to

---

do. He was trying to make art, and if the result was boring, well, at least he'd tried.

Later, Uncle Eddie upgraded to a super-eight camera and gave me his old eight-millimeter. Talk about a door opening. I would take my allowance money and my snow-shoveling money and any other cash I could get my hands on and spend it on film and developing. I filmed my sisters and brothers playing. I filmed our Fourth of July backyard parties. And I made my own attempts at artsy shots. But, whether artsy or everyday, I loved the act of creation— picturing something in my head, trying to capture it on film, and later admiring the result.

Like most people my age, I'd been too focused on today and the future. I'd been guilty of taking Uncle Eddie for granted.

Uncle Eddie died while I was away at college. I didn't even learn of his death until after his funeral. Like most people my age, I'd been too focused on today and the future. I'd been guilty of taking Uncle Eddie for granted. I didn't learn as much from him as I could have. I didn't know him as well as I should have. But, even with my failings, he was an angel to me, helping me find my own way in life. He opened doors for me that I never would have realized existed.

Even when we were just watching the Cubs together.

Sports in my family were seen as pretty frivolous. Life was something to be busy at. You worked. You prepared meals. You sewed clothes. You cut grass. You ran errands. You shopped for groceries. Laziness, for my parents, as for most other survivors of the Depression, was a deep evil.

But in his retirement Uncle Eddie lived what looked like a lazy life, and the laziest of his activities seemed to be watching baseball. What was gained by spending your afternoon in front of the tube, keeping track of the runs, hits and errors? What did you have to show for yourself at game's end? No one actually said any of this to Uncle Eddie, nor did they comment on him to me. But the message was clear in the way people of my neighborhood lived, in how they spent their time.

Uncle Eddie didn't seem to notice that he was listening to a different drummer. He sat there with me watching George Altman run in from center field to snare a line drive or grimacing as Dick Ellsworth gave up a home run in the bottom of the eighth, enjoying himself nonetheless.

Through him I came to understand the meditative nature of baseball. It is a game that moves slowly enough that the viewer has time to think. You have the opportunity to wonder why the manager chose to pinch hit at this particular moment or whether the first baseman should be playing in front of the runner with a left-handed batter now at the plate.

You can, during the pauses between pitches, look out over the vast expanse of the ballpark's grass under the high sky of a summer day and ponder the physical world of God's creation. (Uncle Eddie and I could do this even in his living room, when the images on most televisions were in black and white only.) You can study the faces of the crowd behind the plate or the clothing worn by the fans or the patterns those clothes make in the background.

Watching baseball with Uncle Eddie, I came to realize that life wasn't simply doing. It was also being.

On those afternoons, we didn't worry very much about whether the Cubs would win or lose. (They usually lost.) We weren't concerned about having something to show for our time.

We just were.

> *I need, at the risk of boredom, to be ready to be caught off guard.*

We were there together, sharing mostly in silence an experience. We watched Ken Hubbs and Moe Thacker out on the field, striving to make a hit. And we, in our own way, were striving too. Sitting still, we were taking in a baseball game in all its beauty and its ugliness, ready to be surprised and amazed at some unexpected feat of physical prowess, ready to be puzzled or delighted by a confusing turn of events, ready to catch a glimpse of some inner truth about the game—or about life.

Uncle Eddie taught me many things as we watched baseball together, but the most important is that life is meant to be lived. That means I need to strive to find my way, to listen to what God is calling me to do, to have an impact. But it also means that I need to simply experience life. I need, at the risk of boredom, to sit still, to admire the beauty of the world. I need to take in life, to feel it. I need to be ready to be caught off guard.

The Boys of Spring

by Helen Reichert Lambin

he spring I turned twelve I broke a neighbor's window, almost hit a home run, and learned important lessons about honor, laws of physics, growing old...and boys. This story is set in the mid-1940s in a small town in Iowa (population 4,321, according to the welcome sign at the edge of town).

What we played then could be called sandlot baseball only by the most generous definition. We didn't even *have* a sandlot. Our diamond, to use the word loosely, was the street in front of my yard on a corner lot. We used a regulation-sized softball, not a baseball, but to us we were playing baseball. For one thing, "baseball" probably sounded better to us than "softball." Anyway, I didn't really know the difference between the two at the time.

There were three of us core players, sometimes expanded

by the addition of another boy or two—and they were always boys. I was the only girl who played. There was Tommy, a redheaded, freckle-faced boy straight out of Norman Rockwell. Tommy had come with his mother to live at the home of his grandparents, down the street from me. There was Tommy's sidekick, an amiable boy from Tommy's class at school (the class behind me). Since his name eludes me, we'll call him Bobby. And there was me. I look at a photo from the time, black-and-white, of a dark-haired little girl with a straight bob, looking rather younger than the twelve I must have been.

> It wasn't just that I was a girl, it was that I wasn't an athletically *gifted* girl.

At first the boys weren't too keen on having me join them. It wasn't just that I was a girl, it was that I wasn't an athletically *gifted* girl. I pitched underhand, not over. My hits perversely tended to go foul, although I was a good bunter. I also persisted in saying "catcher's mitt" instead of "fielder's glove." Not that it really mattered, since only one of us had a glove anyway.

On the other hand, I brought certain advantages with me. There were too few players of the right age to begin with, and I was one more person to form a game. I was willing to learn. I generally accepted stoically the sting of catching a ball barehanded, just as the boys did. (And smart it did, sometimes turning your hands red, although I never tested it to the limit by catching a really hard liner.) Whatever I lacked in skill, I made up in enthusiasm. Let other little girls sit around and listen to Frank Sinatra on the Hit Parade. "Batter up, batter up!" was music to my ears.

Oh, and I also owned the only bat.

It was a lovely thing, that bat. My father had taken me uptown to the hardware store to buy it for my twelfth birthday. It wasn't the most expensive bat, but to me it was perfect: smooth, honey-colored, wood gleaming softly from the top to the graceful curve of the barrel to the thin handle with the knob on the bottom. Its weight felt just right to me, and to the boys who envied both it and me.

If there were four or more players, we formed two teams, which we tried to match fairly evenly. If there were only the three of us, as there often were, we played something called "work-up," with its own set of rules that we modified or complicated to fit the requirements of *our* game. Some standard rules we kept, such as three strikes, four balls, and tie goes to the runner. Others were of necessity negotiable—like the number of bases, the fielding positions, and the foul lines.

With one player batting, one pitching, and the third fielding, there was no second batter to bring the runner home. So we eliminated second and third base completely. You rounded first and than ran home. With four or more, we put the other bases back in. The second batter served also as catcher, unless he—or she—got a hit. Then the pitcher moved to cover home.

The game was suspended for passing cars, of course, which fortunately were infrequent on my street, and finally ended when you reached a certain score, number of "innings," or one of us was called home to supper. (Yes, supper. The evening meal was always called supper. "Dinner" or "lunch" was what you ate at noon.)

—

The ironic thing was that on the day I broke the window the game had technically ended. It was one of those glorious Iowa spring days. A soft blue sky dappled with wispy white clouds. A fresh warm breeze carrying the scent of lilac, of freshly cut grass, of spring. And now, through open kitchen windows, came the faint smells of cooking suppers. It was what passed in our neighborhood as rush hour—five or six cars in a half-hour stretch.

We had moved out of the street and onto my front yard grass to throw a few more pitches before supper. I was at bat, three balls, two strikes, with Bobby pitching and Tommy fielding. Then came the moment of truth and glory. I swung and connected. Holy cow, did I connect! It was a Hollywood moment in slow motion, lacking only appropriate music. With a satisfying crack the ball jumped off the bat and soared through the air, white against the blue sky. Tommy faded back to catch it but the ball soared over his head, out of the yard, and across the street.

Even if I had stopped running bases, it would have been a

homer. That is, if the ball hadn't ended its arc with a resounding crash through the neighbor's basement window. We stood for a moment, frozen in place, hoping that maybe it was just a crack, a very loud crack. Then we heard the window shatter and the pieces fall in.

Why—oh, why—hadn't we ended the game in the street?

We looked at one another in silence. Why—oh, why—hadn't we ended the game in the street? And why, if I was going to hit a beautiful homer, did I have to do it then? Dragging my bat. I went in to tell my mother I had just broken the basement window at the Forbes' house across the street.

Swift came the verdict. I would have to go tell Mr. Forbes about the window and offer to pay for it. That was that. It was pretty much what I expected, but awful just the same.

For one thing, there was the "paying for it" part. I suspected my parents would help, but still, where was I going to get any money? (Now, I don't want to do the "In my day we walked five miles to school in winter in our bare feet carrying a turnip sandwich" bit.) Our house was only two blocks from the school and my mother was a good and resourceful cook. But still, this was less than a decade after the end of the Great Depression and within shouting distance of the shortages of World War II. To repeat my father's folk wisdom, "Money doesn't grow on trees, Helen Irene.")

I had the feeling that this could take a lot of pop bottle collecting. For kids too young or too small to baby-sit or mow lawns, there were two primary ways of earning money: running errands for neighbors and collecting pop bottles.

But a broken window? How many pop bottles would that take?

You picked up the glass bottles left out by generous or busy neighbors and returned them to the grocery store for the deposit fee: two cents for the standard size bottles and five cents for the quart size. Given that a candy bar, an ice cream scoop, or a bottle of pop (without the deposit) was then a nickel, this could be a good revenue source. Making a quarter collecting pop bottles wasn't unusual, and occasionally you could top fifty cents or more. Translate that into today's terms and you see that this was not a bad job.

But a broken window? How many pop bottles would *that* take?

To make matters worse, there was facing Mr. Forbes. I had hoped that my mother would do it for me. Or at least *with* me. But no, she said, I had to go myself. True, Mr. Forbes had always seemed a nice, kind-hearted man. But he was one of *them*, a grown-up. More than that, he was *old*. Older than my parents; older than my teacher even. (Good grief, he was very probably even a couple of years older than I am now!)

I went back outside, expecting that the boys would have gone on home by now. After all, I had been the one at bat. I had broken the window. But there were Tommy and Bobby, waiting unhappily in the front yard. I told them what I had to go do. They looked at each other, scuffing their shoes on the ground, as some kind of silent communication passed between them.

"Yeah, okay," they told me. They'd come too...and they'd help pay for the window.

—

Now I have to tell you that this turn of events had never even occurred to me. It was *my* fault, I told them. *I* was the one who had broken the window, not them.

No, they argued in return. These two eleven-year old boys turned out to be men of honor. All three of us had been playing baseball, so it was their fault, too. They were going with me to tell Mr. Forbes. They would help pay for the window. And that was that.

This was one argument in my life that I was happy to lose. Across the street we trudged, the three of us, to knock on the Forbes' back door. It was Mr. Forbes who answered, and we promptly blurted out our story of the breakage and our offer to pay. Mr. Forbes inspected the window and returned to the porch.

"Which one of you broke the window?" he asked.

"I did," I said.

"That must have been quite a hit," he observed. It almost sounded like a compliment. The boys nodded their agreement. "She sure got a hold of that one," Tommy bragged.

I was embarrassed and repeated the part about "pay."

Mr. Forbes shook his head. "It's only a basement window," he said. "Don't worry about it. I'll fix it myself." He paused and smiled—at us, or perhaps at a memory of his own childhood. "You kids may not believe it, but I was young once myself. And I might have broken a window or two."

He turned and went inside, and that, finally, was that. I had won a reprieve, but I had also learned a lesson about boys (and men) and baseball: It can bring out the best in them.

—

This was one of the few times that I have escaped the consequences of my misdeeds. But consequences or not, this was one time that I also learned my lesson—in fact a variety for lessons.

I learned a basic law of physics: When an irresistible force meets an immovable object one or the other of them has to redefine itself.

I learned about the code of honor of being part of a group: Group activities involve group responsibilities—for the *individuals* who make up the group.

I discovered something new about old people: They had also once been young. (Although it would take me several decades before I really believed this truth.) I try to remember Mr. Forbes when someone breaks *my* symbolic windows.

Finally, I learned something about boys: Boys could be

friends with a girl, friends you could count on. It proved to be an invaluable lesson for my years ahead that there was something other than interest, indifference, or dislike that could go on between males and females. There was friendship. In the years to come I would have many boy friends who were not truly *boyfriends*. But I would never have a true *boyfriend* who was not truly a friend.

> *I would never have a true* boyfriend *who was not truly a friend.*

And the man I eventually married was truly my best friend to the end of his life.

———

The year I broke the window was the last spring and summer we played baseball together. That fall I entered junior high and Tommy moved away from our street. By the time I was in high school, I knew that what we called baseball was actually softball. And softball was one more boring thing required of girls in gym class. It was something totally different from those free form, free-spirited, *fun* games I had played with the boys of spring.

Baseball was not big in Iowa back then. The games that really mattered in high school were football and, above all, basketball. For four years I dutifully went to (well, most of) the home games because it was the socially acceptable thing to do. But once I grew up and moved to Chicago I decided—and publicly stated—that I had seen enough spectator sports to last a lifetime and that never again would I go to a game just to please a boy.

And I never did, until the boy in question was my son.

—

I did, once, several decades later, make a perfect catch to parallel my perfect hit. It was winter now, not spring, and I was leaving school after chaperoning a cadre of sixth grade boys on a field trip to the zoo.

Suddenly I felt a change in the air. I turned to see a snowball hurtling toward me. I reached up with one mittened hand (think *fielder's glove*) and caught the snowball in flight. The boys stared open-mouthed in surprise. I casually brushed my mitten off and left the field for home.

I remember thinking, *It's too bad the boys of spring couldn't have seen what the boys in winter just saw.*

I still don't go to ball games. And I still say, if asked, that I saw enough games back in high school to satisfy any interest in sports. This is still true for football and basketball. But I'm not so sure about baseball.

Maybe on those first warm spring days, before the heat of summer, when the breeze is soft and carries a hint of spring, maybe when the inning ends and the new pitcher steps up to the mound and the outfielders fade back into position, maybe then the next batter up should be me.

Looking for the Story Line

by Michael Wilt

hea Stadium, 1982. I'm a young, green catcher, called up from the Mets Triple A farm team in the middle of a muggy June homestand. An injury to the starting catcher has made my promotion necessary. The team's second catcher will do an adequate job of filling in, but he needs a break, so on this lazy Sunday afternoon, a day game after a night game, he gets his rest and I make my debut in the bigs. No expectations. Just filling a need for a mediocre team that will finish, at best, in the middle of the pack.

I make my presence known in the top of the first inning when Pete Rose of the Phillies doubles and then tries to score on a single to right. A perfect throw arrives at the same time as Rose, but I am ready—braced, blocking the plate, and giving no ground as we collide. The ball stays in my glove as Rose crumples away from me. The umpire calls "Out!" and I reset myself to throw to third if the trailing base runner dares try to advance from second. Time is called, I flip the ball to my pitcher and gather my wits. "Welcome to the big leagues, Rook," I hear Rose say as he dusts himself off and heads to the dugout. I smile and give him a look, but wait till his back is turned before I shake the cobwebs from my head, feeling lucky to be alive.

~

Okay, that scene never really happened. But sometimes as I'm falling asleep at night I like to imagine myself two and a half decades younger than I am today, playing baseball in the major leagues.

This is not simply a matter of watching myself, in my sleepy mind's eye, take some cuts against Nolan Ryan. Nor is it a matter of imagining my career listing in *The Bill James Handbook*—tiny, dry numbers on thin, white paper. What I am looking for as I attempt to nod off is a story line, and baseball always has a story line—from pitch to pitch, out to out, run to run, inning to inning.

> What I am looking for as I attempt to nod off is a story line, and baseball always has a story line.

I love that about baseball—story lines: stories of second and third chances, of letdowns and comebacks, of goats today who are heroes tomorrow; stories of players who get it done on the field and then show up at a schoolyard or playground to make a difference in the lives of some kids; stories of guys who make it very big and then fall very far, subject like the rest of us mortals to human foibles and weaknesses and addictions; stories that ain't over till they're over, and even then....

We live and learn by stories. We can't escape them. All of our religious traditions are infused with stories—Moses on Mt. Sinai, Jesus at a wedding, Mohammed at Mecca. And the stories don't stop. The Christian story, for example, tells of the life and teachings of a controversial public figure, with little stories strung together throughout: healings and miracles and parables and conversations and encounters. It goes on to tell of an execution and a surprising resurrection.

Every time we hear a story it takes on new shades of meaning. Stories never freeze or calcify—they are dynamic, and unless we as hearers are made of stone, we should never hear them the same way twice.

—

I've made two trips to the National Baseball Hall of Fame and Museum in Cooperstown, New York, and I hope to go there again before too long. It's a marvelous brick building, with well-appointed and thoroughly documented exhibits. Included, of course, are classic artifacts of baseball associated with some of the most storied people and places of the game.

On my first trip, I lingered near any exhibit having to do with Willie Mays, like the glove he was wearing when he made "the catch" in game one of the 1954 World Series between the Giants and the Indians. That game was played at the Polo Grounds, two years before I was born. The Polo Grounds was a classic and quirky ballpark now lost to history, but at the Hall you can bring it back to the present as you stand beside turnstiles from the entrance to the park.

I never saw Mays and the New York Giants play there, but the Mets played two seasons in the Polo Grounds, and that's where I saw my first major league game. I was about six years old. My father and brother and I saw Willie Stargell and the Pirates beat Casey Stengel's Mets 10 to 3 on a sunny summer afternoon. We sat on the first base side, beneath the overhanging seating level above us. It was as if we were watching the game from inside a cave, complete with stalactite-stalagmite iron support girders interrupting the view at regular intervals. The memory is like a fuzzy dream story in the background of my consciousness, but there it is, filed under "First Major League Baseball Game," subheading "Polo Grounds," sub-sub-heading "I Actually Saw a Ballgame at the Polo Grounds!" Perhaps, I thought, as I stood beside the exhibit at the Hall of Fame, I walked through one of these very turnstiles . . . perhaps.

During that trip to Cooperstown, I purchased two tee shirts featuring a beautiful graphic of the Polo Grounds—the kind of drawing that brings a long lost place back to life. I gave one to my father and kept the other for myself. I wore mine and washed it and wore it and washed it out of existence; I'll have to check with my dad and see if he still has his.

The part of the museum that I found least interesting was the Hall of Fame itself, the mausoleum-like room that houses all of the Hall of Famer plaques. The room is a monument to baseball's greatest, designed—ironically—to inspire hushed reverence for men who played a boys' game in front of raucous unruly crowds. In contrast, the history of baseball is best captured in the rest of the museum, where the stuff of story lives.

Maybe I'm just not the hushed reverence type, and I can live with that. In the thirty years since my grandmother's death, for example, I have not visited her grave. But I frequently think of her: how she raised her two sons alone without complaint, never thinking of herself as a "victim" of divorce; and of the summer trips she took with my siblings and me; and how the last time I saw her alive, three weeks before she died, she gave me an envelope containing a hundred dollars so I would have some cash in my pocket for my first semester of college. The monument to her that counts to me is not the granite one in a green field in New Jersey, it's the elements of character that were sown in me by knowing her for eighteen years and hearing and telling stories about her at holiday dinners and during long-distance phone conversations with the folks back home.

Memories and the ways to honor them come in many varieties.

Physical monuments have their place. Memories and the ways to honor them come in many varieties. For the most part, though, I'll continue to prefer the memory rooms in which I can virtually hear the crowd and smell the hot dogs and see the faces that have brought meaning to my life.

About twenty years ago I went to a Mets-Pirates game that lasted eighteen innings. At the end of the first inning, you would have guessed that the story of the game would be that Darryl Strawberry hit the first grand slam homer of his career—an opposite-field chip shot that appeared to have no chance to clear the left field fence. By the end of the eighteenth, however, there were too many stories to count: Pirates' pitchers coming up to bat as pinch hitters; Clint Hurdle and Rusty Staub exchanging places in right and left field depending on the batter; the aging, never-was-fast-in-the-first-place Staub making the catch of his life after the sprint of his life. The game included an amazing array of scoring chances, all missed until the bottom of the eighteenth when Hurdle drove in pinch-runner Mookie Wilson without getting credit for either a hit or a sacrifice (the Pirates' first basemen couldn't handle a routine grounder). Despite losing, the Pirates out-hit the Mets 18 to 6. It was a very unusual game in which just about anything that can happen in a baseball game did happen. Just about anything that could have gone wrong, went wrong. Purists

Purists who love the perfectly executed hit and run or sacrifice fly or timely hit or managing-by-the-book would not have loved that game.

who love the perfectly executed hit and run or sacrifice fly or timely hit or managing-by-the-book would not have loved that game. But it was a great game for us storytellers.

Storytellers thrive on quirks and imperfections and surprises and sudden shifts of perspective. Storytellers resist the temptation to burden a simple plot line—for example, "Christ has died; Christ is risen; Christ will come again"— with extreme tangents of dogma, doctrine and rules for membership. They can handle the notion that profound truth can sing from a story that does not necessarily contain a single fact, and need not rationalize miracles, strange plot twists, or "difficult sayings" via science, theology, or blind faith. Telling a story invites the listener to enter the story and make it his or her own. Telling a story encourages the listener to assimilate the principles behind the action into his or her life. Telling a story engages the emotions and intellect of the listener and inspires questioning, argument and deeper inquiry.

The writers of the Gospels were among the first to tell the story of Jesus, and I doubt that any of them believed that what they had done was definitive. They knew they had not said the last word about the God-man who had walked among them and their forebears. They would be peeved, I am sure, if they knew that the story has been largely taken away from raconteurs and instead chiseled into stony sermons and vapid greeting card slogans and static doctrinal statements that read as poorly and incompletely as the thumbnail summaries of out-of-town ballgames in *USA Today*: bereft of nuance, heart, poetry—bereft, in fact, of their story line.

I try to enter into the Jesus story in the same way I enter into a ballgame. Live the moments of redemption—redemption big and small, not just the "capital R" redemption of the catechism writers. The strikeout swing this inning is a home run swing in the next; the scorned tax collector hosts dinner for God-with-us. The base runner and the shortstop salute each other after a hard slide at second base; the "unclean" woman's flow of blood stops when she touches the hem of his garment. The player who commits the error in the field knocks in two runs in his next at-bat; the disciple who denied he knows his Master is given the charge to "Feed my lambs."

Stories like these can inspire devotion. But there is another way to respond, and that is to internalize the trajectories of the lives depicted in the stories. From lost to striving, from ailing to healing, from doubtful to certain, knowing all the while that there is no guarantee we won't slide back or go into a slump—I think that's called "keeping the faith," and I think it's the most challenging and necessary form of devotion.

Anyone who has ever coached young ball players knows

how hard it is to keep kids "in the game" through the ups and downs of hits and strikeouts and errors and great throws. I've coached my son, Sam, along with other boys and girls, and I've tried to impress upon them that what signifies success and failure in baseball is the same as what signifies success or failure in life: It is about making stories and keeping the faith.

A kid is on hands and knees in the batter's box. He was just hit in the back with a pitch. You rub his back, let him know it's okay to cry, and tell him slyly, "By tomorrow morning this'll be a great story for you to tell." Each time he tells it, or just thinks about it (because we think in stories), he'll get up to the plate again despite the failure or pain. In so doing, he'll be keeping the faith.

I like to remind Sam about an at-bat last season, one in which he displayed the kind of determination a father likes to see in his kids: "You had a count of no balls and two strikes practically before you stepped into the batter's box. I shouted to you to protect the plate. You fouled off four or five close pitches. In between, you let one, two, three balls sail by outside the strike zone. 'Good eye, good eye,' I yelled, and finally you held back from swinging at ball four and walked to first. You were on the brink of an out but you fought through it and walked to first base. You kept the faith, pal. Now *that's* baseball."

And that's life.

Baseball is played on a field in the shape of a diamond. Foul lines mark the boundaries of the game, and grandstands and fences mark the boundaries between players and fans. But no true fan leaves the power of baseball back behind those fences when the game is over. He or she takes it home, in story and laughter and tears, and tells it just a bit differently each time. Our stories matter. They are in our blood and DNA; they make us human. We've just got to let them burst out into our days and nights. "Keep looking for the story line," I'll continue to tell my son. "The stories are what make us real."

It's a Team Effort

by Jean Larkin

ut, Mom, they *need* me," I remember pleading in my most pitiful ten-year-old voice. My mother was at work, and I was calling to beg for permission to stay after school and play in the fourth-grade Sacred Heart girls' softball game.

Teams were not "official" in the sense that there was an organized league with formal registrations. No one even wore a uniform, yet everyone knew these girls represented our school and were therefore very important people.

Sister Mary Philip was the coach—a scrappy, barely-five-foot-tall, black-robed ball of fire whom everyone with any sense feared. Her temper was quick and fierce, as reknowned as her ability to smack the ball over the fence and to shout down anyone for any reason at any time.

I was new to the school and had never played on the team, but I had played as much sandlot ball as most ten year olds, not with any particular distinction, mind you, but at least I knew the rules and could get the ball from second to first without it flying wildly over the first baseman's head.

For some reason I no longer remember, the regular second baseman for Sacred Heart could not play that day, and I'm sure it was only because the word *forfeit* was not in Sister Mary Philip's vocabulary that she "scouted" me at recess that morning. "Tell your mother we need you," she said as she ushered me across the street to use the phone at Sophie's Confectionary.

> It was at that moment—the first ever of which I remember being aware—that I felt the least bit important and, well, necessary.

Now that particular moment in my life would certainly not have registered as significant to anyone at the time, least of all me. Yet I can still smell the sweet mix of candy and cakes and bubble gum in Sophie's. I can still feel my sweaty palms and see the jet blackness of the phone receiver with my fingers curled around it in a grip that said "the harder you hold on, the more likely Mom will say yes."

Mom really didn't need this unexpected kink in her tightly-scheduled day, which always began early and ended late, as every "working Mom's" day did. "But, Mom, they *need* me," I said again when I sensed her hesitancy, and it was at that moment—the first ever of which I remember being aware—that I felt the least bit important and, well, *necessary*. After all, if Sister Mary Philip said I was needed, it must be so. No one disputed the word of Sister Mary Philip, not even God, as far as I knew, and certainly not my mom. She caved, and I could play.

Surely there are impressive psychological and theological terms for that brief moment when we experience a spiritual awakening. I don't know what those terms are, but I do know that hearing (and believing) three very simple words "they need me" gave my self-image and feeling of self-worth a little kick-start into life.

—

No flashes of profound insight made themselves known to me that day, but from my present vantage point of adulthood I recognize that moment in Sophie's Confectionary as a key one in my relationship with God and my fellow human beings. I had taken a baby step toward seeing myself as a unique creature, someone who was part of a team—an important part, a *necessary* part.

From fourth through eighth grade, I continued to play softball on the Sacred Heart girls' teams. I have no memories of any other particularly significant developments in my psyche or in the blossoming of my relationship with God. This would certainly be a better story if I could say that my experience that day led me to a life of fame and glory in the world of sports. But I never progressed much beyond my skills as a ten year old.

I do believe, however, that because of that brief moment with Sister Mary Philip of feeling sure the game could not go on without me, baseball has always held a special significance for me. My feeling of importance that day came from a confidence not based on any fact, for most likely Sister had already been turned down that day by every other fourth-grade girl and would have asked some third-grader to play if I couldn't. I wasn't *really* irreplaceable, but that didn't matter. It mattered that I believed I was.

Baseball Lesson for Life #1: Each of us is necessary and needed. Life is a team effort.

—

Perhaps because of that early positive baseball experience, I believe that God has continued to use that glorious sport to teach me important life lessons that have all reinforced in some way that first lesson. For example, another key moment in my "game of life" came some twenty years later when my own son was playing baseball in grade school. I was now one of those faithful parents who blessed the person who thought of weaving plastic strips together into a chair and then figured out how to fold it so it could be carried at all times in the trunk of a car.

My chair and I attended all my son's games and formed alliances with other folding-chair-toting parents. We were polite, civilized people, but we also were clear about our devotion to our respective teams. The parents from the competing team sat "over there" and we sat "over here."

Ned joined my son's team in fifth grade. He was the tallest, most athletic-looking kid on the team. His first appearance at the plate in every game forced fielders to back up and coaches to start shifting their players into positions for what would most likely be a hard hit, long ball.

> *I've often wondered what kept him coming back. Surely he wasn't getting a boost in his self-image each time he swung and missed.*

But Ned was in fact the most uncoordinated boy on the team. Game after game he struck out in each at-bat, hardly ever making contact with the ball at all. Opponents got to know him and learned to pretty much ignore any threat they once felt from him. Parents from the competing team no longer let out loud "oohs" of fear when they saw Ned approach the plate. We faithful followers, however, continued to encourage Ned with each at-bat: "This one's yours, Ned. You can do it."

Ned persevered with baseball through sixth, seventh and eighth grade, each summer growing taller and more formidable looking. Yet each season produced no progress in his coordination. I've often wondered what kept him coming back. Surely he wasn't getting a boost in his self-image each time he swung and missed. Could he really be having fun out there? Whatever it was, I admired him for sticking with it, although I resigned myself to another loss whenever Ned came up to bat with the game on the line.

Through the years of watching one another's sons make

progress with their fielding, pitching and hitting skills, we parents from the various schools in the area all pretty well knew which boys were capable of what. We remained competitors, urging our own boys on to victory as loudly as we could, but something had gradually changed through the years. It showed up in small ways: When one of the players committed an especially embarrassing error, no matter which team the boy was on, both sides of the field would join the chorus of "Just shake it off." When a boy got up limping after sliding into base, we'd ask about him after the game, even if he was on the other team. To me, the most obvious change was when Ned came up to bat, struck out, and went back to the bench.

After a while, the competing parents no longer cheered for their team's good fortune.

After a while, the competing parents no longer cheered for their team's good fortune. I wondered if it was because they now considered him no threat or if this was just another example of the "softer, gentler" competitors into whom we all had evolved.

Our coach was a patient, encouraging guy who made sure every boy played no matter what. So of course Ned came up to bat at least once in every game. Then one game in the eighth grade, when the season was almost over, Ned came to the plate. We parents started our usual banter of "This one's yours, Ned. You can do it."

To everyone's astonishment, Ned's bat connected with the first pitch. Whack! Just like in the movies, that ball flew way over the outfielder's head, who was playing in, of course, because it was only Ned up there. Ned took off running and we parents went wild, cheering him around each base until he actually made it all the way home. Unbelievable! Ned had his first hit ever and it was a home run.

We couldn't stop cheering, but gradually I realized that the rousing cheers for Ned were not all coming from our side of the field. The parents of the boys on the other team—who had all watched Ned struggle for four years, who admired his determination, who must have been silently rooting for him to get at least one hit in his young life—were all standing and yelling, "Way to go, Ned! We knew you could do it!"

I have no doubt that God was cheering for Ned, but I'm also sure that there were some divine "way to goes" for us parents on both sides who, along with Ned, were experiencing a key moment in our lives. For a good team effort, it is important for all of us to know and feel that we are necessary and needed, but it is as important to know that we need every other person on the team as well.

Baseball Lesson for Life #2: None of us wins if we root only for our side. Life is a team effort—on both sides of the field.

Sometimes God teaches us a life lesson during a quiet and private moment, like the one I had in fourth grade. Sometimes we experience them among a group of others sharing the same experience with us, like the parents cheering together for Ned. Sometimes we learn just by watching.

Major league baseball players (like most professional athletes) are so closely monitored when they are participating in their sport that almost every moment of their performances is captured on film or broadcast over the airwaves or sent into cyberspace to become a part of the universe's "permanent stats." Every moment, whether it is key to them personally or not, is out there for all to see—and see again and again on instant replay and highlight reels.

I love going to the St. Louis Cardinals' games. It's great to be part of the crowd and feel the energy of the team right there in front of you. But I can't get to many of them, so I see most games on television. I'm always a bit amazed and sometimes annoyed that whether a player is on the field or not, he is fair game for the cameras. They catch the guy doing something he'd probably rather not have broadcast on television—mundane things like getting a drink or ill-mannered things like spitting or scratching himself in unflattering places. The point is it has nothing to do with who he is or his ability to play the game, but the cameras roll anyway. There must be times a player thinks, "Why does everything I do have to be recorded?"

But I witnessed what I'm sure was a key moment in one young father's life that involved a major league pitcher and, no, it was not captured on national television nor did it warrant a radio interview or a photograph in the paper. One and only one time in my life, thanks to a combination of someone's generosity and a dash of my own good luck, I was blessed with an invitation to sit in a front row seat at a Cardinals' game. Our seats were right behind the Cardinal dugout—pure heaven for anyone who wants to see her heroes up close. Naturally there are a lot of people in the stadium who are in that category, and many of them are young and determined and armed with pens and paper and ball gloves. Our section was prime territory for getting autographs, as well as catching foul balls that had been touched by an actual real live major league player.

I thoroughly enjoyed each play of the game from my privileged vantage point.

The ushers were evidently instructed to herd the kids away at game time and not to allow them back until after the game ended, because during the game we who were lucky enough to be in those seats were not to be disturbed by the autograph seekers, and we weren't.

I thoroughly enjoyed each play of the game from my privileged vantage point, and the day ended perfectly with a Cardinal victory. As the players ran off the field toward the dugout, however, the kids flocked down again to the front row to try to catch the attention of the players. I have to admit I was a little irritated by having my special space invaded.

Among the mob was a young man holding his son, who was probably about three years old. The little boy had a too-large baseball cap on his head, a too-large ball glove on his hand, and a wide-eyed look of wonder on his face. It turned out that the Cardinal ace pitcher, Matt Morris, who had not pitched that day, had sat through the game in the dugout. Those of us behind the dugout, of course, didn't know this, because you can't see who's in there until they walk out.

As the players ran in from the field, Morris stepped out of the dugout and looked at the group assembled there. They all started calling his name to get his attention and win his favor. He graciously smiled and waved at everybody. Then he saw the father and son. He pointed to the man and indicated that he'd be right back. I guess the rest of the autograph seekers didn't realize this, because their interest scattered in other directions as soon as he disappeared into the dugout again. But the father and son stayed put. Some minutes passed, and I assumed that Morris wasn't coming back after all. I could see that the father was thinking the same thing. He was of course disappointed and started telling his son, "Well, maybe next time."

Then he saw the father and son. He pointed to the man and indicated that he'd be right back.

Suddenly Morris reappeared, this time with a ball in his hand. The kids all swarmed back, but Morris held his hands up and said, "Hold on a minute." Then he indicated to the kids to stay back, he pointed to the little boy, and he rolled the ball slowly across the top of the dugout so that the little boy could "catch" it in his glove. What a look of joy on the faces of both the father and the son, and I'll admit that my own face had tears rolling down it.

Was this a sacred moment? Maybe not for Matt Morris, but probably so for the dad and his son. Surely it was for me, because I had just witnessed one of the most famous pitchers in baseball help another man feel special. It wasn't a public relations setup for the media. There was no paid endorsement deal. It would not help advance Morris' career or reputation one whit. But I'm sure it meant the world to that father and son.

I've heard that Matt Morris is a really nice man, so he's probably done things like that after many games. He most likely doesn't even remember the day I'm talking about. But on that day, in that moment, he sent a message that two people were valued and important.

Baseball Lesson for Life #3: It is not enough to recognize that we are special, or even to remind ourselves that others are special. We must let others know that they are special. Life is a team effort.

—

I have no idea how many key moments occur in our lifetime, but I know that every day we provide key moments for one another—whether it's at home or work, in church or the mall, on the schoolyard or the baseball diamond. We've all been picked for the team. We all get our turns at bat. Sometimes we hit the ball out of the park. Sometimes we miss it altogether. Sometimes we give it to a little boy. But it's important that we all stay in the game, because we can't win without one another.

Life is a team effort.

Epiphany
in Saint Louis

by William John Fitzgerald

A boy's will is the wind's will,
and the thoughts of youth are long, long thoughts.
William Wadsworth Longfellow

First of all, I remember the sandlots: "Hey, throw that bat in the air and let's choose sides!"

That's the way it was always done sixty years ago.

The bat went up and one of the two "captains" (usually the oldest and most skilled boys among us) would grab it. Then hand over hand the captains worked their way up the narrow neck of the bat to see who could get the last minimal piece of flesh to touch the top of the bat and thus have the first choice in the selection of players.

I was usually chosen last.

I also remember the "thud" the ball made when it was hurled into the catcher's mitt. (Yes, we actually used the words *hurled* and *hurler* back then, and we called the catcher's mitt a *pud*.)

I remember the crack of the bat when an old, beaten-up

wooden "Louisville Slugger" lofted the ball beyond the left fielder, occasionally followed by the sickening sound of breaking glass when the ball went just a little too far into someone's yard.

But most of all, I remember my dad.

—

"Hey Dad, can we play catch after supper?" I'd plead almost every night when he got home from his office job at the Union Stock Yards.

He never said no. I'd pretend I was a pitcher and hurl the ball (see, I told you we used the word) with all my might. Not that there was any danger of hurting my dad's hand. I was a scrawny, skinny kid—uncoordinated and awkward. So I had to pretend that I was Bob Feller or Dizzy Dean. Dad and I both knew the unspoken reality: I would never ever play baseball for any real team. The best I could do was throw him the "high heat" in our back yard, which was good enough for both of us.

Dad and I both knew the unspoken reality: I would never ever play baseball for any real team.

In traditional rites of passage in many cultures, it is the father who leads the son out of childhood into the adult world. My father surely knew that he was not leading me, his only son, into a career as a ball player. He knew because he had been a fair high school athlete himself. He had to realize that I lacked the talent to play baseball beyond the sandlot. Yet he provided me the opportunity to imagine that I could.

In doing so, Dad *did* lead me to allow my imagination to flourish, and *that* would become the talent I would develop throughout my life as a priest, preacher, storyteller and author.

When I was growing up, big league games were broadcast exclusively by radio. So not only did I have to imagine myself as a pitcher, I also had to imagine what a big league game actually looked like. All I had to go on were the scenes described by someone sitting at a microphone far away. Those of us without access to a major league city could only dream about seeing "real baseball" with our own eyes.

But in my teen years it came to pass that my father was able to provide his only son with a glimpse of the great beauty that is major league baseball. One day he announced, "Let's drive down to St. Louis and see a real live big league ball game!"

I assumed I was actually going to get to see "Stan The Man" Musial and the St. Louis Cardinals—the closest thing to a big league "home team" in Omaha where we lived. When my father tried to coincide his vacation time with the major league schedules, however, he discovered the Cardi-

---

nals would be on the road at the time that we would be in St. Louis. My heart sank, but then Dad told me, "We won't be able to see the Cardinals, Billy, but there's another team in St. Louis—not as glorious as the Cards, but still a genuine big league team—the St. Louis Browns. They are playing the Philadelphia Athletics, and I'm sure Connie Mack will be there. He started managing the A's way back in 1901. He's the grand old man of baseball."

So I would see two major league teams, even if they were in the "junior circuit" American League. Dad explained to me that it was a big deal to get a glimpse of one of the patriarchs and legends of baseball—Cornelius Alexander McGillicuddy—nicknamed Connie Mack.

Never mind that the Browns were the perennial cellar dwellers in the American League, and the A's were used to being there too. Big league baseball was still big league baseball, and I was going to be there.

―

I can remember my excitement building as we drove into Saint Louis and found our way to a night game at the old Sportsman's Park. As I write now, Sportsman's Park is long gone—as are the St. Louis Browns. But all I cared about then was that it was a major league stadium. Dad assured me that it even had a grass infield, which seemed incomprehensible to a boy used to playing his games exclusively on sand lots where a blade of grass was an endangered species.

There were no parking lots in those days; or at least we couldn't find one. So Dad pulled up in front of a house in the neighborhood and paid a youngster a quarter to "watch our car." We arrived early for the game, and after we moved through the turnstiles, Dad asked if I would like to buy a baseball hat.

Now I have had many wonderful moments in my life, but at that point I did not think that life could get much better than this. "Sure, that would be great, Dad!" I said.

"Well, which team's hat would you like—the A's or the Browns?" he asked.

Since I had always been a scrawny kid, prone to being picked on at school, I kind of thought of myself as an underdog.

Since I had always been a scrawny kid, prone to being picked on at school, I kind of thought of myself as an underdog, although one day—through some very surprising moves on my part—I had actually thrown a bully to the sidewalk at school. So choosing this hat took on special significance for me. I knew these were two "bad" teams and it was a close call which one was the bigger underdog. I liked the color brown, however, so after a brief moment of indecision (with my dad being patient as he always was) I decided that the Browns would be my chosen underdog—for the game we were about to see and probably for the rest of the season and maybe even my life. (I have since gone on to be a Chicago Cubs and an Arizona Diamondbacks fan, so most of my life has in fact been spent cheering for underdogs.)

The vendor handed me a St. Louis Brown official baseball cap. I looked at it carefully. The felt cap part was a dark brown with a lighter colored button on top. The visor was burnt orange and on the front was emblazoned a scripted "S" embroidered with a scripted "L."

More than half a century later I can remember the scene vividly.

As I fit that cap on my head, my excitement was building to the breaking point. We made our way to the ramp leading us into the stadium. For me it was like entering a great, long tunnel that would end in heaven itself. More than half a century later I can remember the scene vividly: As we emerged from the darkened tunnel, there before me was a big league diamond flooded with bright lights for the night game. The infield was framed by red dirt, and—sure enough—the infield was a vibrant green carpet that looked as if it had never been stepped on. Most of the stadium was painted a dark blue that contrasted beautifully with the green grass.

Players were warming up—the Browns in their cream uniforms edged in brown and burnt orange, the Athletics clad in gray flannels. And there, straight across the field from me, sat an elderly man in a blue business suit. He had a high starched collar—the kind that went out in the twenties—and wore a white Panama hat. Although he was no longer the manager, he sat on a chair next to the A's dugout with a scorecard in his hand. My eyes were like saucers when my father turned and whispered to me, somewhat in

            Diamond Presence

awe himself, "See him over there? That's the great Connie Mack."

—

As a teenager, I did not know what an "epiphany" was, but I do now. My entrance into that ballpark was an experience so luminous that it hinted at divine glory. Phil Cousineau, in his book, *Once and Future Myths: the Power of Ancient Stories in Modern Times*, describes a similar memorable experience he had with his father during his first visit to the old Detroit Tiger stadium in 1963.

That particular game at Tiger stadium stands out in bas-relief for him compared to the hundreds of other sports experiences with his father. It was so luminous for him that it possessed "transcendent possibilities."

I can declare my first moments at Sportsman's Park that summer evening became an epiphany for me. After all, what is an epiphany if not an experience that goes so far beyond the normal and ordinary events of human existence that it gives us just a hint of the source of all beauty and light—a reality that we believers call "God"?

Epiphanies are not just for emperors or saints, they do not occur only on mountaintops or in mangers. They can be experienced by all of us—even a teenager with his dad at a ballpark.

The sight of Connie Mack and that beautiful stadium was not the end of my epiphany. As the game was about to begin, the announcer made a special announcement over the loudspeakers: "Ladies and gentlemen, we call your attention to the box next to the Athletics dugout. We have the great honor to have present with us this evening, along with his wife and their son, the General of the Armies of the United States of America, General Douglas MacArthur!"

Suddenly the mass of humanity rose as one and gave the great World War II hero a round of applause. I remember thinking, "Wow, baseball must *really* be important if even General MacArthur would take the time to come to a game."

I do not remember who won. The score was not that important to me. Hardly anyone alive today remembers much about the St. Louis Browns. They were in decline on their way to extinction, but fortunately I didn't realize it that night. Their one claim to fame had been in 1944, when most of the great ball players in the major leagues were in the service. That year, for the only time, the Browns won the American League pennant. In 1945 they were contenders again, but after that it was all down hill.

Still, they managed a few memorable moments in baseball history. In 1945, the Browns put the first one-armed baseball player on the field. His name was Pete Gray and he played seventy-seven games that year. In 1951, Bill Veeck, who had first signed Satchel Paige to pitch for the Cleveland Indians, brought him to the Browns, allowing one of the greatest pitchers of all time to continue to play in the major leagues where he had always belonged.

Douglas MacArthur "faded away" as he said old soldiers always did.

That same year Veeck also hired a midget named Eddie Gaedel. On August 18, Veeck suited up the three-foot-seven, sixty-five pound Gaedel in a tiny Browns' uniform with the numeral 1/8 on the back. Then he sent Gaedel in as a pinch hitter against the Detroit Tigers. He was walked on four consecutive pitches and never played another game. (Veeck was severely reprimanded by the baseball commissioner and a rule was put in place to prevent something like this from ever happening again.)

As I reflect back on this wonderful baseball experience from my youth, I wonder why it has stuck with me so strongly over all the years. Douglas MacArthur "faded away" as he said old soldiers always did. The Browns and Sportsman's Park are long gone, and the A's are in Oakland, not Philadelphia.

But it was neither Connie Mack nor General MacArthur nor the Browns nor the A's who provided me with my epiphany. It was Bill Fitzgerald, my father, the one who took the time to play catch with me in our yard and allowed my imagination to flourish. It was my dad who led me out of the dusty sandlots into the bigger world of major league baseball and from there to the world of adulthood. He led me through the narrow tunnel at Sportsman Park and opened up to me the luminous experience that is life.

Babe Ruth Blesses the Sons of Kerry

by Carol DeChant

Always, spring has meant baseball in Iowa. Our oldest family documents tell of games played on the farm after Sunday Mass.

Grandfather Graney hosted those games in the orchard. His land was part of over 2,300 acres my great-grandparents had eventually accumulated after fleeing Ireland's famine. Dad was born on that Iowa soil, where the sons of County Kerry played ball.

The games ended in the 1920s, after the fire. A family historian wrote that the Ku Klux Klan burnt my grandfather's farmhouse, along with those of his two brothers. Dad, who was a boy then, remembers watching the flames from town, but says he never heard the adults discuss the cause of the fires.

———

Mom died last October, shortly after my parents' seventieth anniversary. Now, in the spring of 2003, Dad longs to see gardens and crops again, and for the solace of baseball. For Dad, finding that solace depends upon looking beyond the mania for new measures of performance that is everywhere this season.

I get hooked into debates about whether on-base percentages are better indicators of pitchers' skills than the old win-loss records. I join stat-obsessed fans who focus on team payroll budgets. Doesn't it stand to reason that the Yankees, with the highest team payroll of $180 million, will win the World Series? I fret about the Cubs' mid-level $83 million payroll.

Iowans are by nature and by geography minor league fans, unconcerned with the big money obsessions of the majors.

Such tortured computations are beside the point to Dad. Iowans are by nature and by geography minor league fans, unconcerned with the big money obsessions of the majors. Our attention is now on this season's high traffic between the AAA Iowa Cubs and the Chicago team due to injuries. Choi, Patterson, Sosa, Grudzielanek, Prior…have so many stars ever been injured so early in a season?

From my home in Chicago, I talk to Dad about these struggles. One Cubs game that goes seventeen innings reminds Dad of a Des Moines double-header he saw in 1925. Pat Malone pitched the entire first game and into overtime in the second one. "Malone was on the mound for twenty-three innings," Dad says. "Can you imagine today's players doing that? Then getting on a bus to another town and pitching again the next day?"

Appreciation for Malone's feat has grown over the decades since Dad witnessed it. He doesn't remember who won either game, because the score is never Dad's point. He does recall that Malone went up to Chicago after that, and pitched ten years in the big leagues.

—

This spring Dad becomes a patient himself, after many years of caring for Momma. My sisters and I had been there last fall when a hospice nurse guided our parents through Momma's final weeks.

Dad has also outlived medical care as he had once practiced it as an osteopathic surgeon. He had lectured on the art of diagnosis, but now the lack of success in discovering the cause of his pain cost him days and nights of misery. After he emerges from this ordeal, he tells me why the medical team took so long to diagnose his condition: "They were studying their charts rather than their patient." Medicine, like baseball, is all about the numbers these days.

Dad's own numbers are monitored daily now. But he has always known that the measure of a man isn't given in milligrams and cc's. Nor do scans or sonograms depict the whole person. Unable to measure grief, they may even fail to tell you what's wrong with him.

Baseball is a welcome distraction from all of this. Chicago goes on a spending spree, buying new players who brilliantly plug holes left by the injured stars. Late summer is electrified with near no-hitters, split-second double-plays, and crackerjack batting. Heading into Labor Day weekend, I see the Cubs as contenders for their first World Series win in ninety-five years.

Dad doesn't dwell on my playoff predictions, however. His attention is on the game of each day. At ninety-two, a baseball fan lives for the sacrifice of the present moment. Nurses come into Dad's room and find him watching WGN-TV. "What's the score, Doc?" they ask. Dad replies, "I don't know the score, I'm watching the *game*."

———

Cleaning out our parents' apartment after Dad's move to the nursing home, I find three sports pages he has held onto throughout his life.

On May 3, 1930, the Des Moines *Register* headlined: "Baseball Under Lights Proves a Success Before 12,000 Fans." A reporter describes the thrill of that first night game (I notice that the writer shares Dad's priorities—the score is secondary):

"One hundred and forty-six projectors diffusing 53,000,000 candlepower of mellow light and the amazing batting of Des Moines' nocturnal-eyed players made the opening of the local baseball season a complete success. Baseball was played successfully after dark on an illuminated field and [Des Moines] won, 13-6, in a contest that was normal in every respect so far as the playing was concerned."

Bleacher fans arrived early, "carrying blankets and lunches" to be there the moment the lights came on. Night games went on to become the salvation of baseball during the Great Depression.

Dad had once told me that the Bambino had visited his alma mater, St. Patrick's School in Perry, Iowa.

Babe Ruth is the subject of Dad's other clippings. Dad had once told me that the Bambino had visited his alma mater, St. Patrick's School in Perry, Iowa. The *Perry Daily Chief* from October, 1922, tells about Ruth and Bob Meusel joining local teams for a game. Playing for Pella, Meusel hit a home run, but Ruth led Perry to a 12-4 victory. Ruth and Meusel were guests at a Knights of Columbus dinner that night.

In an era when the "antipapist" KKK was expanding rapidly, a visit from America's hero was an unparalleled morale boost for the parochial school kids. A history book helped me put Ruth's visit in the context of that day's anti-Catholicism. *A Town Called Perry* describes local KKK initiations. One was preceded by a parade of 500 Klansmen "in full regalia.... Fiery crosses furnished the light, and drum-and-bugle corps the marching music. A minister...gave the address." A newspaper reports that the town's first Klan funeral was attended by 1,500 friends of the deceased. (Perry's population in that era was only 5,642).

The Klan made a clean sweep of the local 1924 election. Clearly, their presence was felt. The cause of our family's fires was never reported, but a cousin tells me the KKK burnt a cross in St. Pat's church yard.

Yet the Perry newspaper, which offered "just the facts" reports of Klan activities, was enthusiastic about Ruth: "There is perhaps no person...mentioned in print more often than Babe Ruth...the hero of every red blooded American lad...." the front-page said.

Babe offered comeuppance to his era's bigots.

All Americans knew Babe Ruth's record then. But Catholics also knew his story: how the Xaverian Brothers had discovered and nurtured his ball playing talent when he was in their orphanage. Babe offered comeuppance to his era's bigots, and Dad's yellowed clippings confirm that baseball's best stories are not statistical ones.

—

But these old stories are forgotten as the Cubs make it to the playoffs. They triumph against Atlanta. Next, they return to Wrigley Field up three games to one against the Marlins, a wild card team whose manager was dumped mid-season. *Statistically*, I tell Dad, it is impossible for Chicago *not* to win the pennant: We need only one more win. In three games. Starting two of them are Wood and Prior—the best pitchers by any measures. At home. Against the Marlins. Whose new manager is a seventy-two-year-old grandfather called out of retirement to resuscitate a dying team.

The Cubs, on the other hand, have Dusty Baker, who leads us into the final play-off games with unprecedented confidence. Instead, we come out to face a long winter asking "What happened?" Perhaps as good an answer as any is that the stats can lie.

For me, the season is thrilling and heartbreaking and ultimately unbelievable, not unlike life. Baseball's new math tempted me to believe that we could see farther and deeper than ever before; October reminds me what Dad knew all along—that most teams lose, that every player's numbers eventually tank. My father's final cherished newspaper is a 1948 story about Ruth retiring his number at Yankee Stadium.

Between the last two Cubs losses, Dad tells me he feels better than he has in over a year. His thoughts of Momma focus more on their earlier days now, long before hospice. Mine do too. Maybe emerging from loss is a process of righting the balance of our memories, restoring the better ones along with the worst. Spring and summer and this baseball season have helped us do that.

My father told me about Babe Ruth's visit years ago, but I have a better grasp now of all it meant. For on that one day, the KKK stashed their sheets to cheer alongside the Catholics, who claimed America's hero as one of their own. Among them was Dad, at age twelve.

No doubt baseball has helped lift other families up too, given them something to talk of when there was nothing more to say about their sorrows. It has surely also united other communities in bad times, as it did that day in Dad's home town. The newspaper story about Babe Ruth's visit is Perry's most requested archive, an Iowa historian tells me. Even eighty years later, families want to preserve that memory.

What hasn't been preserved as winter approaches is last spring's mania about new percentages. The playoff team with the lowest budget won the Series, making those big money theories as quaint as that 1922 paper boasting that Ruth and Meusel left Perry "with the big end of the $1055 gate receipts."

This season's truth tells a whole different story, one that Dad has always appreciated: the worth of a player and a team is shown on the field, in the play of the moment. Statistics only tell you what happened yesterday, and payroll budgets based on them can't predict tomorrow's heroes. You don't play baseball on paper. Thank goodness. That would be like trying to put a price on Babe Ruth's visit.

Or on sharing another baseball season with your ninety-two-year-old dad.

Under the Lights

by Andre Dubus

he first professional baseball players I watched and loved were in the Class C Evangeline League, which came to our town in the form of the Lafayette Brahman Bulls. The club's owner raised these hump-backed animals. The league comprised teams from other small towns in Louisiana, and Baton Rouge, the capital. The Baton Rouge team was called the Red Sticks. This was in 1948, and I was eleven years old. At the Lafayette municipal golf course, my father sometimes played golf with Harry Strohm, the player-manager of the Bulls. Strohm was a shortstop. He seemed very old to me and, for a ballplayer, he was: a wiry deeply tanned graying man with lovely blue eyes that were gentle and merry, as his lined face was.

Mrs. Strohm worked in the team's business office; she was a golfer too, and her face was tan and lined and she had warm grey-blue eyes with crinkles at their corners. In the Bulls' second season, she hired me and my cousin Jimmy Burke and our friend Carroll Ritchie as ball boys. The club could not afford to lose baseballs, and the business manager took them from fans who caught fouls in the seats. No one on the club could afford much; the players got around six hundred dollars for a season and when one of them hit a home run the fans passed a hat for him. During batting practice we boys stood on the outside of the fence and returned balls hit over it, or fouled behind the stands. At game time a black boy we never met appeared and worked on the right field fence; one of us perched on the left, another of us stood in the parking lot behind the grandstands, and the third had the night off and a free seat in the park. Our pay was a dollar a night. It remains the best job I ever had, but I would have to be twelve and thirteen and fourteen to continue loving it.

During batting practice we boys stood on the outside of the fence and returned balls hit over it.

One late afternoon I sat in the stands with the players who were relaxing in their street clothes before pre-game practice. A young outfielder was joking with his teammates, showing them a condom from his wallet. The condom in his hand chilled me with disgust at the filth of "screwing," or "doing it," which was a shameful act performed by dogs, bad girls, and thrice by my parents to make my sisters and me; and chilled me too with the awful solemnity of mortal sin. That season, the outfielder was dating a young Catholic woman, who later would go to Lourdes for an incurable illness; she lived in my neighborhood. Now, recalling what a foolish boy the outfielder was, I do not believe the woman graced him with her loins any more than baseball did, but that afternoon I was only confused and frightened, a boy who had opened the wrong door, the wrong drawer.

Then I looked at Harry Strohm. He was watching the outfielder, and his eyes were measuring and cold. Then with my own eyes I see the outfielder's career as a ballplayer. He did not have one. That was in Harry's eyes, and his judgment had nothing, of course, to do with the condom: it was the outfielder's cheerful haplessness, sitting in the sun, with no manhood in him, none of the drive and concentration and absolute seriousness a ballplayer must have. This was not a professional relaxing before losing himself in the long hard moment-by-moment work of playing baseball. This was a youth with a little talent, enough to hit over .300 in Class C, and catch fly balls that most men could not, and throw them back to the infield or to home plate. But his talent was not what Harry was staring at. It was his lack of regret, his lack of retrospection, this young outfielder drifting in and, very soon, out of the profession that still held Harry, still demanded of him, still excited him. Harry was probably forty, maybe more, and his brain helped his legs cover the ground of a shortstop. He knew where to play the hitters.

My mother and father and I went to most home games, and some nights in the off-season we ate dinner at Poorboy's Restaurant with Harry and his wife. One of those nights, while everyone but my mother and me was smoking Lucky

---

Andre Dubus   145

Strikes after dinner, my father said to Harry: My son says he wants to be a ballplayer. Harry turned his bright eyes on me, and looked through my eyes and into the secret self, or selves, I believed I hid from everyone, especially my parents and, most of all, my father: those demons of failure that were my solitary torment. I will never forget those moments in the restaurant when I felt Harry's eyes, looking as they had when he stared at the young outfielder who, bawdy and jocular, had not seen them, had not felt them.

—

I was a child, with a child's solipsistic reaction to the world. Earlier that season, on a morning before a night game, the Bulls hosted a baseball clinic for young boys. My friends and I went to it, driven by one of our mothers. That was before seatbelts and other sanity, when you put as many children into a car as it could hold, then locked the doors to keep them closed against the pressure of bodies. By then I had taught myself to field ground and fly balls, and to bat. Among my classmates at school, I was a sissy, because I was a poor athlete. Decades later I realized I was a poor athlete at school because I was shy, and every public act—like standing at the plate, waiting to swing at a softball—became disproportionate. Proportion is all; and, in sports at school, I lost it by surrendering to the awful significance of my self-consciousness. Shyness has a strange element of narcissism, a belief that how we look, how we perform, is truly important to other people.

In the fall of 1947 I vowed—I used that word—to redeem myself in softball season in the spring. I used the word *redeem* too. We had moved to a new neighborhood that year, and we had an odd house, two-storied and brick, built alone by its owner, our landlord. It had the only basement in Lafayette, with a steep driveway just wide enough for a car and a few spare inches on either side of it, just enough to make a driver hold his breath, glancing at the concrete walls rising beside the climbing or descending car. The back wall of the living room, and my sisters' shared bedroom above it, had no windows. So I practiced there, throwing a baseball against my sisters' wall for flies and against the living room wall for grounders. In that neighborhood I had new friends and, since they did not know me as a sissy, I did not become one. In autumn and winter we played tackle football, wearing helmets and shoulder pads; when we weren't doing that, I was practicing baseball. Every night, before kneeling to say the rosary then going to bed, I practiced batting. I had learned the stance and stride and swing from reading John R. Tunis's baseball novels and from *Babe Ruth Comics*, which I subscribed to and which, in every issue, had a page of instructions in one of the elements of baseball. I opened my bedroom door so the latch faced me, as a pitcher would. The latch became the ball and I stood close

> I practiced there, throwing a baseball against my sisters' wall for flies and against the living room wall for grounders.

enough to hit it, my feet comfortably spread, my elbows away from my chest, my wrists cocked, and the bat held high. Then one hundred times I stepped toward the latch, the fastball, the curve, and kept my eyes on it and swung the bat, stopping it just short of contact.

> *The two captains chose teams and, as always, they chose other boys until only two of us remained.*

In the spring of 1948, in the first softball game during the afternoon hour of physical education in the dusty schoolyard, the two captains chose teams and, as always, they chose other boys until only two of us remained. I batted last, and first came to the plate with two or three runners on base, and while my teammates urged me to try for a walk, and the players on the field called "Easy out, Easy out," I watched the softball coming in waist-high, and stepped and swung, and hit it over the right fielder's head for a double. My next time at bat I tripled to center. From then on I brought my glove to school, hanging from a handlebar.

That summer the Bulls came to town, and we boys in the neighborhood played baseball every morning, on a lot owned by the father of one of our friends. Mr. Gossen mowed the field, built a backstop, and erected foul poles down the left and right field foul lines. Beyond them and the rest of the outfield was tall grass. We wore baseball shoes and caps, chewed bubble gum and spat, and at the wooden home plate we knocked dirt from our spikes. We did not have catcher's equipment, only a mask and a mitt, so our pitchers did not throw hard. We did not want them to anyway. But sometimes we played a team from another neighborhood and our catcher used their shin guards and chest protector, and we hit fast balls and roundhouse curves. I don't know about my other friends, but if Little League ball had existed then I would not have played: not with adult coaches and watching parents taking from me my excitement, my happiness while playing or practicing, and returning me to the tense muscles and cool stomach and clumsy hands and feet of self-consciousness. I am grateful that I was given those lovely summer days until we boys grew older and, since none of us was a varsity athlete, we turned to driving lessons and romance.

There were three or four of those baseball seasons. In that first one, in 1948, we went one morning to the Bulls' clinic. The ball field was a crowd of boys, young ones like us, eleven or twelve, and teenagers too. The day began with short drills and instruction and demonstrations. I don't remember how it ended. I only remember the first drill: a column of us in the infield, and one of the Bulls tossing a ground ball to the first boy, then the next boy, and so on: a fast, smooth exercise. But waiting in line, among all those strangers, not only boys but men too, professional ballplayers, I lost my months of backyard practice, my redemption on the softball field at school and the praise from my class-

mates that followed it, lost the mornings with my friends on
our field. When my turn came I trotted toward the softly
bouncing ball, crouched, took my eyes off the ball and saw
only the blankness of my secret self, and the ball went
between and through my legs. The player tossed me another one, which I fielded while my rump puckered as in antic-
ipation of a spanking, a first day at school. Harry Strohm
was watching.

So later that summer, amid the aroma of coffee and tobacco smoke at the table at Poorboy's, when he gazed at me
with those eyes like embedded gems, brilliant and ancient, I
saw in them myself that morning, bound by the strings of
my fear, as the ball bounced over my stiffly waiting gloved
hand. Harry Strohm said nothing at the table; or, if he did,
I heard it as nothing. Perhaps he said quietly: "That's good."

I was wrong, and I did not know I was wrong until this
very moment, as I write this. When Harry looked at me
across the table, he was not looking at my body and into my
soul and deciding I would never be a ballplayer, he was not
focusing on my trifling error on that long day of the clinic.
He was looking at my young hope and seeing his own that
had propelled him into and kept him in this vocation, this
game he had played nearly all his life. His skin was deeply,
smoothly brown; the wrinkles in his face delineated his
skin's toughness. He wore a short-sleeved shirt and slacks. I
cannot imagine him in a suit and tie, save in his casket; cannot imagine him in any clothing but a baseball uniform, or
something familiar, something placed in a locker before a
game, withdrawn from it after the game and the shower,

some assembly of cotton whose only function was to cover his nakedness until the next game, the next season. He had once played Triple A ball.

———

So had Norm Litzinger, our left fielder. A shoulder injury was the catalyst for his descent from the top of the wall surrounding the garden where the very few played major league baseball. I do not remember the effect of the injury on his performance in the Evangeline League. Perhaps there was none, as he threw on smaller fields, to hold or put out slower runners, and as he swung through pitches that most major leaguers could hit at will. *He was brown, and broad of shoulder and chest, handsome and spirited, and humorous.* He was fast too, and graceful, and sometimes, after making a shoestring catch, he somersaulted to his feet, holding the ball high in his glove. Once, as he was sprinting home from third, the catcher blocked the plate. Litzinger ducked his head and ran into the catcher, who dropped the ball as the two men fell; then Litzinger rose from the tumble and dust, grinning, holding his shoulders sloped and his arms bent and hanging like an ape's, and walked like one into applause and the dugout.

He was in his thirties. At the end of every season he went home, to whatever place in the North. For us, everything but Arkansas above us was the North; everything but California, which was isolated and odd. One season he dated a beautiful woman who sat with another beautiful woman in a box seat behind home plate. I was thirteen or fourteen. Litzinger's lady had black hair and dark skin, her lips and fingernails were bright red, her cheeks rouged. Her friend was blond, with very red lips and nails. They both smoked Chesterfields, and as I watched them drawing on their cigarettes, marking them with lipstick, and blowing plumes of smoke into the humid and floodlit night air, and daintily removing bits of tobacco from their tongues, I felt the magical and frightening mystery of their flesh. The brunette married Norman Litzinger; and one night, before the game, the blonde married Billy Joe Barrett with a ceremony at home plate.

The brunette married Norman Litzinger; and one night, before the game, the blonde married Billy Joe Barrett with a ceremony at home plate.

One season I read a book by Joe DiMaggio. I believe it was a book of instruction, for boys. I only remember one line from that book, and I paraphrase it: If you stay in Class D or

C ball for more than one season, unless you have been injured, you should get out of professional baseball. Perhaps DiMaggio wrote the word *quit*. I can't. I've spent too much of my life in angry dread of that word.

How could I forget DiMaggio's sentence? I loved young ballplayers who, with the Bulls, were trying to rise through the minor leagues, to the garden of the elect. I loved young ballplayers who, ~~like the outfielder with the condom~~, were in their second or third seasons in Class C ball. And I loved old ballplayers, like Harry Strohm and Bill Thomas, a fifty-year-old pitcher with great control and an assortment of soft breaking balls, who one night pitched a no-hitter; and once, when because of rain-outs and doubleheaders, the Bulls had no one to pitch the second game of a double header, he pitched and won both of them. And I loved players who were neither old nor young, for baseball: men like Tom Spears, a pitcher in his mid-twenties, who had played in leagues higher than Class C, then pitched a few seasons for us on his way out of professional baseball. He was a gentle and witty man, and one morning, because we asked him to, he came to one of our games, to watch us play.

Late one afternoon Mrs. Strohm gave both my cousin Jimmy and me the night off, and we asked the visiting manager if we could be his batboys. Tom Spears pitched for the Bulls that night. This was a time in baseball when, if a man was pitching a no-hitter, no one spoke about it. Radio announcers hinted, in their various ways. Fans in seats looked at each other, winked, raised an eyebrow, nodded. We were afraid of jinxing it; and that belief made being a fan something deeper than watching a game. An uninformed spectator, a drunk, even a thirteen-year-old boy could, by simply saying the words *no hitter*, destroy it. So you were connected with everyone watching the game, and everyone listening to it too, for a man alone with his radio in his living room, a man who lacked belief, could say those two sacred words and break the spell.

But Jimmy and I did not know until the night Spears pitched a no-hitter, while we were batboys for the New Iberia Pelicans, that the opposing team transcended their desire to win, and each player his desire to perform, to hit, and instead obeyed the rules of the ritual. We were having fun, and we were also trying to do perfect work as batboys; we did not know Spears was pitching a no-hitter. We sat in the dugout while the Pelicans were in the field, sat with pitchers and the manager and reserve ballplayers. When the Pelicans were at bat we stayed close to the on-deck circle, watched hitter after hitter returning to the dugout without a hit. And no one said a word. Then the last batter struck out on a fastball, a lovely glint of white, and the crowd was standing and cheering and passing the hat, and the Bulls in the field and from the dugout were running to the mound, to Spears. Then the Pelicans were saying the two words, surrounding them with the obscenities I first heard and learned from ballplayers, and they went quickly to their bus—there were no visiting locker rooms in the league—and left their bats. Jimmy and I thrust them into the canvas bat bag and ran, both of us holding the bag, to the parking lot, to the bus. The driver, a player, had already started it; the team was aboard. "Your bats," we called; "Your bats." From the bus we heard the two words, the obscenities; a player reached down through the door and hoisted in the bag of Louisville Sluggers.

——

How could I forget DiMaggio's sentence? Our first baseman, in the Bulls' first season, was a young hard-hitting lefthander whose last name was Glenn. We were in the Detroit Tiger system, and after Glenn's season with us, he went up to Flint, Michigan, to a Class A league. I subscribed to *The Sporting News* and read the weekly statistics and box scores, and I followed Glenn's performance, and I shared his hope, and waited for the season when he would stand finally in the garden. At Flint he batted in the middle of the order, as he had for us, and he did well; but he did not hit .300, or thirty home runs. In the next season I looked every week at the names in *The Sporting News*, searched for Glenn in double A and triple A, and did not find him there, or in Class A or B, and I never saw his name again. It was as though he had come into my life, then left me and died, but I did not have the words then for what I felt in my heart. I could only say to my friends: I

> *It was as though he had come into my life, then left me and died, but I did not have the words then for what I felt in my heart.*

can't find Glenn's name anymore.

I believed Billy Joe Barrett's name would be part of baseball for years. I believed he would go from us to Flint, then to double and finally triple A, and would have a career there, at the top of the garden wall. And, with the hope that is the essence of belief, I told myself that he would play in the major leagues; that one season, or over several of them, he would discover and claim that instant of timing, or that sharper concentration, or whatever it was that he so slightly lacked and that flawed his harmony at the plate. In the field he was what we called then a Fancy Dan. He was right-handed and tall, fast and graceful and lithe. He leaped high and caught line drives as smoothly as an acrobat, as though the hard-hit ball and his catching it were a performance he and the batter had practiced for years. On very close plays at first, stretching for a throw from an infielder, he did a split, the bottom of one leg and the top of the other pressed against the earth; then quickly and smoothly, without using his hands, he stood. He stole a lot of bases. He often ended his slide by rising to his feet, on the bag. He batted left-handed and was a line drive hitter, and a good one; but not a great one.

I have never seen a first baseman whose grace thrilled me as Barrett's did; and one night in Lafayette he hit a baseball in a way I have never seen again. He batted lead-off or second and every season hit a few home runs, but they were not what we or other teams and fans or Barrett himself consid-

> *In the field he was what we called then a Fancy Dan.*

ered either a hope or a threat when he was at the plate. But that night he hit a fast ball coming just above his knees. It started as a line drive over the second baseman, who leaped for it, his gloved hand reaching up then arcing down without the ball that had cleared by inches, maybe twelve of them, the glove's leather fingers. Then in a short right field the ball's trajectory sharply rose, as though deflected higher and faster by angled air, and the right fielder stopped his motion toward it and simply stood and watched while the ball rose higher and higher and was still rising and tiny as it went over the lights in right field. Billy Joe Barrett's career ended in Lafayette.

—

How could I forget DiMaggio's sentence? Before I got out of high school, the Bulls' park was vacant, its playing field growing weeds. The Strohms had moved on, looking for another ball club; and Norm Litzinger and Billy Joe Barrett and their wives had gone to whatever places they found after Lafayette, and after baseball. I was driving my family's old Chevrolet and smoking Lucky Strikes and falling in love with girls whose red lips marked their cigarettes and who, with painted fingernails, removed bits of tobacco from their tongues; and, with that immortal vision of mortality that youth holds in its heart, I waited for manhood.

DiMaggio was wrong. I know that now, over forty years after I read his sentence. Or, because I was a boy whose hope was to be a different boy with a new body growing tall and fast and graceful and strong, a boy who one morning would wake, by some miracle of desire, in motion on the path to the garden, I gave to DiMaggio too much credence; and his sentence lost, for me, all proportion, and insidiously became a heresy. Which I am renouncing now, as I see Billy Joe Barrett on the night when his whole body and his whole mind and his whole heart were for one moment in absolute harmony with a speeding baseball and he hit it harder and farther than he could at any other instant in his life. We never saw the ball start its descent, its downward arc to earth. For me, it never has. It is rising white over the lights high above the right field fence, a bright and vanishing sphere of human possibility soaring into the darkness beyond our vision.

Burying Maris

by Jerome D. Lamb

The flags of North Dakota, by order of the Governor, flew at half mast the day they buried Roger Maris. St Mary's Cathedral, seat of the Bishop of Fargo, suspended the Christmas season for a day, taking down its giant advent wreath so that the television cameras in the choir loft could get a better angle on the funeral proceedings below. And even the weather, operating under the direction of yet higher authorities, became moderately cooperative; after days below zero the temperature climbed to six above, and a gentle, post-card pretty snow came down, white and clean and peaceful.

Not many if, ands or buts about it, it was a very big deal up here, the burying of Roger Maris. Not only because many celebrated boys of summers past—a Mike (Shannon), a Mickey (Mantle), a Moose (Skowron), two Whities (Ford and Herzog), assorted Bobbies (Richardson and Allison) and a Clete (Boyer)—had come to town to bear the pall, nor because a wave of nostalgia had splashed across the snow banks with such force that even the achievements of the local Bison, North Dakota State University's football team, fresh from winning their second NCAA Division II Championship in three years, got swept away in the reminiscences of middle-aged men, every third one of whom seems to have played some sort of ball—foot, base or basket—with or against old Rog in days longer gone by than we had remembered. No, there was more to the week than all that; there was something else, having to do with the realization that *he* was being buried *here*, that after all this time, all those days in the sun and nights under the lights, this frozen piece of earth perched on the near side of nowhere was still and always home.

> *There was something else, having to do with the realization that he was being buried here.*

Perhaps we have probably just assumed that major leaguers were automatically interred in spring training land—Florida or California or Texas, somewhere somewhat summery. We assume a lot of things up here, many of them based on the premise that no one much knows we exist, or cares.

Which is okay most of the time, at least to everyone but the Chamber of Commerce drumbeaters: we know it's good country, weather notwithstanding, but we don't expect anyone else to know. We've long since adjusted to living in fly-over land, grown used to being patronized by short term residents on their way to somewhere else—to the home office in Peoria, the bigger, better college in Ohio, the classier life in Seattle. We stay and amuse ourselves by ticking off the names of those who have passed through—Bob Dylan was here a week or two, Dustin Hoffman a couple of months, Peggy Lee a year or more. They don't come back, but that's all right; we shrug and bow to the inevitable—talent never stays.

Which isn't true of course. There are talents and talents; some flourish in the quiet places, and others where the spot lights shine, where all the glory is. And that isn't here, North Dakota being singularly short on spotlights and mega-phones, and somewhat long on admiration for the effects those machines can create. We make do with the quiet tal-ents—the mechanic who knows at first hearing that what's in order is a minor adjustment, not a major overhaul, the piemaker at such and such a café, the trapper who could track a weasel across the asphalt of a shopping mall parking lot if he had to.

Still, because we're human, as exposed to the subtle influ-ences of *The Tonight Show* and the *National Enquirer* as people in Biloxi or the Bronx or Butte, we tend to be mightily impressed with officially designated stars, people whose tal-ents, less useful maybe but more showy, have been approved by experts from elsewhere. So the mechanics and the piemakers and the plain folk who somehow caught the knack of living the good life get buried without much fan-fare; fine people, salt of the earth and all, but too much like us, not quite like them.

Maybe the significance of the Maris burial was that it somehow bridged the gap between "us" and "them." He was certainly one of them, the superb athlete whose gifts—
strength, speed, stamina, grace and a dozen other things—

*He came from
here, and he
came back here.*

were meant to bloom in a bigger garden than we have around here, with a
longer growing season. But still he was
part of here. For years Roger Maris has
remained a distinctly un-asteriskable
presence in Fargo, as real as the March
Blizzard of 1941 or the 1957 Torna-
do—part extraordinary natural phenomenon, part myth,
and part something uniquely the region's own. A kid who
wandered down these streets, who turned his collar up
against the wind in winters much like this, who went up
against the best of them and did damn well. Never mind the
Hall of Fame committeemen; never mind the fickleness of
fans and scribes and pundits and various national know-it-
alls. Never mind the reticence that was billed as truculence,
the outdated crewcut, the old-fashioned life style. When we
get down to what it's all about, which we sometimes do at
funerals, those things don't matter much; what matters is
what's been done with what we had. And on those green
fields of the earth where the good eye and the good swing
and the good arm and the stout heart are the things that

count, are the tools of the trade, Roger Maris excelled. And he came from here, and he came back here, and that is significance enough.

It was a big funeral, but not fancy. Old ballplayers, old fans, old friends; a Mass and the long ride out to the home field. In New York a few days later there was a memorial service at St. Patrick's; Roger wasn't there, but a lot of *People* people were: George Steinbrenner, Ed Koch, Peter Ueberroth, Richard Nixon, Howard Cosell and the like. At the end of the Mass, John Cardinal O'Connor, a cover story churchman, called for applause; the crowd stood and clapped for a full minute, probably with more restraint than if the cathedral had been Yankee Stadium, but heartily, lustily even. It was a nice New York touch, but somehow it seemed to us that the soft snow on the quiet earth out here was a nicer touch. Applause fades after all; the earth endures.

Heaven Begins
on the Spot
Where You're Standing

by Michael Leach

eaven begins on the spot where you're standing. Baseball teaches you that.

Long before Eckhart Tolle wrote *The Power of Now*, baseball taught me that God comes to us when we least expect it: in the present moment.

I first knew God (without knowing I knew God) playing softball. It took only a moment. And then it was gone.

—

I was eight or nine years old. Maybe ten. It doesn't matter. Because when it happened, time stood still and I was eternal.

In my big-city neighborhood the kids played softball on cross streets where manhole covers served as bases. The fourteen-incher was popping its stitches, and you used it until it was a pillow. Even so, you'd better not smack it too far down the middle or it might crack the window of an apartment building. You had to pull the ball to the street on the left or punch it down the street on the right. You began playing after school and didn't stop until your mother called your name from a wooden porch or the sun sank behind the skyline.

Little guys like me sat on the curb until one of the big guys had to go home.

Little guys like me sat on the curb until one of the big guys had to go home. Then they'd put us in, usually on the street to the right. I'd often drop the ball, especially hard line drives, and rarely hit one past the pitcher. I wanted to do good (or more accurately, not do bad) and thought about what the other kids were thinking of me. Then one evening (or more accurately, one timeless moment) while the sun was painting the apartment windows gold, I stopped wanting, stopped thinking.

And heaven said hello.

I was in right field. The ball popped off the bat like grease from a frying pan and lofted high over my head. All I did was see it and turn and follow its path. I wasn't thinking about it. Just running, aware of each step, each move of my arms, as if in slow motion, knowing exactly where the ball would come down. At just the right moment, without looking, my fingers reached out and the softball fell onto my hands like a dove. I ran a few more steps, turned, held it up, and smiled.

The big guys cheered.

The moment vanished.

But to this day, more than fifty years later, I can remember that golden instant, when time stood still and I felt one with the ball, the sun, the street, and, yes, let's say it, love.

Baseball teaches us simply to pay attention to the ball.

God is love, and love is an unbelievable oneness that comes to awareness when you least expect it: *in the present moment*. Baseball teaches us not to worry about the past or plan the future but simply to pay attention to the ball. And sometimes, when we do—when we give up wanting and not wanting—heaven begins to happen.

I don't remember what happened after that catch, but I remember other sacred moments in my life that came when I least expected them but that never lasted more than an inning. Just as quickly as one came, just as quickly would I take pride in it or dwell on it or try to do it again, and it was gone.

In *Cyrano*, the poet says,

There comes a moment to everyone
When beauty stands staring into the soul
With sad, sweet eyes that sicken at the sound of words,
And God help those who pass that moment by.

Michael Leach   171

Baseball, at its best, represents a moment of grace when you forget about yourself and live in the present. Awareness catches *you*, but the moment passes by when you try to pin it against the wall of your mind like a butterfly. It comes to you, on colorful see-through wings. And as soon as you take credit for it, it vanishes.

But you never forget it.

Its promise keeps you going.

You don't have to play baseball to find yourself by losing yourself. For those of us who have, however, baseball lets us know: Heaven begins on the spot where you're standing.

About the Contributors

Carol DeChant is the author of *Momma's Enchanted Supper: Stories for the Long Evenings of Advent*. She is a contributor to *Christmas Presence* and splits her time between Chicago and Florida.

Andre Dubus was the author of numerous books and the winner of many awards, including the PEN/Malamud Award, the 1997 Rea Award for excellence in short fiction, the Jean Stein Award from the American Academy of Arts and Letters, the *Boston Globe's* first annual Lawrence L. Winship award, grants from the National Endowment for the Arts, two followships from the Guggenheim Foundation, and a major grant from the MacArthur Foundation. He died of a heart attack in his home in Haverhill, Massachusetts, on February 24, 1999.

William John Fitzgerald is the author of *A Contemporary Celtic Prayer Book, Seven Secrets of the Celtic Spirit*, and many other books. A priest of the Diocese of Omaha, Nebraska, he is retired and living as the "author in residence" at Our Lady of Perpetual Help parish in Scottsdale, Arizona.

Patrick Hannon, CSC, a Holy Cross priest, is the Director of Mission Effectiveness for Notre Dame High School in Chicago, Illinois and the author of a book of stories about prayer to be published by ACTA Publications. He is a contributor to both *Christmas Presence* and *Hidden Presence*.

Sara Kaden is an editor for WSA Corp. in Kansas City, Missouri, and is working on a forthcoming biography of Lou Gehrig. She maintains a Baseball Hall of Fame-recognized

Website, www.MoreGehrig.com, dedicated to her personal hero.

Jerome D. Lamb is a retired librarian in Fargo, North Dakota. He has been the editor and publisher of *The Small Voice* for over twenty-five years.

Helen Reichert Lambin is a retired college administrator in Chicago and the author of *The Death of a Husband* and *From Grief to Grace*. She is a contributor to *Hidden Presence*.

Jean Larkin works in St. Louis, Missouri, as the editorial director of Pflaum Publishing Group. She is a former editorial director of Liguori Publications and has edited hundreds of books and articles.

Michael Leach is the publisher of Orbis Books in Maryknoll, New York, and lives in Riverside, Connecticut. He is the co-author of *I Like Being Catholic* and *I Like Being Married* and a contributor to both *Christmas Presence* and *Hidden Presence*.

Robert Raccuglia is the director of the Cenacle Retreat and Conference Center in Chicago and the former executive director of Serra International. He is a contributor to *Hidden Presence*.

Patrick T. Reardon is a reporter for the *Chicago Tribune* and the author of *Daily Meditations (with Scripture) for Busy Dads* and *Starting Out: Reflections for Young People*. He is a contributor to *Christmas Presence* and *Hidden Presence*.

Michael Wilt is the editorial director of Cowley Publications in Cambridge, Massachusetts. He maintains the Website www.nimblespirit.com, dedicated to literature and spirituality.

Acknowledgments

ou cannot compile a collection of great original stories unless you know a lot of great storytellers. Fortunately, I do.

Thanks to Carol DeChant, Bill Fitzgerald, Pat Hannon, Sara Kaden, Helen Lambin, Jean Larkin, Mike Leach, Bob Raccuglia, Pat Reardon and Michael Wilt—first for being my friends and colleagues and secondly for sharing their baseball stories with me and with you. Special thanks to Fr. Patrick Samway, S.J., for putting me in touch with Patricia Dubus, the daughter of Andre Dubus, who graciously gave permission to include "Under the Lights" in this collection, and to Jerome D. Lamb for allowing me to publish "Burying Maris" for the first time in book form.

I also want to thank John Dewan, my partner at ACTA Publications, for contributing the Foreword and for his unwavering support. Special thanks to Carol DeChant, who helped conceive of this book and collaborated with me on it every step of the way.

The stories in the three *Presence* books to date have all served to remind me of the truth I first learned at Mother of Sorrows grammar school in Rochester, New York: We don't have to get away from our daily lives to find God; God is always there, just waiting for us to notice. As Mike Leach puts it, "Heaven begins on the spot where you're standing."

And finally to you, dear reader, I offer my sincere appreciation. For a book is truly complete only when someone has read it from the beginning to the end.

If you enjoyed *Diamond Presence*, you might also like the award-winning books *Christmas Presence: Twelve Gifts That Were More Than They Seemed* and *Hidden Presence: Twelve Blessings That Transformed Sorrow or Loss*, both published by ACTA Publications. Contributors include Carol DeChant, Patrick Hannon, Helen Reichert Lambin, Michael Leach, Robert Raccuglia, Patick T. Reardon and other great spiritual writers. Both *Christmas Presence* and *Hidden Presence* are published as $17.95 hardcover books with gift ribbons. They are available at bookstores or by calling 800-397-2282 or at www.actapublications.com.